ALPHABET SOUP

ALPHABET SOUP

a memoir in letters

A. GREGORY FRANKSON

RARE MACHINES

This is a work of personal memoir that reflects the author's present recollections of experiences over time. Names and characteristics of persons and places have been changed; some events have been compressed or time frames otherwise adjusted; some dialogue and interactions have been creatively reformulated; and the author acknowledges that the recollections of others about the persons or events described may differ.

Publisher: Meghan Macdonald | Acquiring editor: Kwame Scott Fraser | Editor: Peter Midgley
Cover and interior designer: Laura Boyle
Cover image: Letter collage assembled from images and textures on Unsplash contributed by Bernard Hermant, Aneta Pawlik, Meric Dagli, and Alice Donovan Rouse.

Library and Archives Canada Cataloguing in Publication

Title: Alphabet soup: a memoir in letters / A. Gregory Frankson.
Names: Frankson, A. Gregory, author.
Identifiers: Canadiana (print) 2024042395X | Canadiana (ebook) 20240426878 | ISBN 9781459750333 (softcover) | ISBN 9781459750357 (EPUB) | ISBN 9781459750340 (PDF)
Subjects: LCGFT: Literature.
Classification: LCC PS8611.R3627 A79 2025 | DDC C816/.6—dc23

We acknowledge the support of the Canada Council for the Arts and the Ontario Arts Council for our publishing program. We also acknowledge the financial support of the Government of Ontario, through the Ontario Book Publishing Tax Credit and Ontario Creates, and the Government of Canada.

Printed and bound in Canada.

Rare Machines, an imprint of Dundurn Press
1382 Queen Street East
Toronto, Ontario, Canada M4L 1C9
dundurn.com, @dundurnpress

For Doreen Lorraine Frankson Jones

You taught me to read. You taught me to dance.
By doing so, you taught me to live.

I love you, Mom, more than words could ever hope to say.

For Carmen Carric-Gatesy (1952–2023)

I am so grateful that you showed me what life lived
in poetic prose looked like up close. I am honoured
beyond words that you called me your son.

Love you, Mama. Salut!

For the thirty people who are the subjects
of the letters in this book:

"Ingratitude is sooner or later fatal to
its author." — Twi proverb

Author's Note

There are twenty-six written letters in this book. Each one, addressed to a letter of the alphabet, is composed with a specific state of being, emotion, or character trait in mind to thematically frame the letter's content. The letters comprise a variety of interpretations of the moments, relationships, occurrences, and observances I've experienced, and are placed in an order that reflects the randomness the human journey can bring.

The letters are written in poetic prose, both for the expressive freedom it provided but also as a transition from the purely poetic expressions that I primarily worked with prior to the development of *Alphabet Soup* to a deeper exploration of topics that seemed suited to prose rather than poetry. The opportunity to do this kind of writing felt like a healing journey in phrase, imagery, and metaphor. My wish is that these letters will cause readers to reflect on a phrase or image that evokes feelings of nostalgia or brings a treasured remembrance to mind.

The order of the letters was generated using the random.org List Randomizer website back when I first conceived of this project in 2018. I entered the twenty-six letters of the alphabet, in order and one per line, into the input box. For the purposes of the book, I liked the symbolism of beginning with the letter *i* (which is where I believe every self-examination should begin), and so I hit "randomize" a few times until the first time the letter *i* came up in the first position. This result became the sequence in which the letters appear in this book.

Yet random order does not necessarily mean entirely random randomness. The themes and topics in these letters fold back into each other in the way lines, images, and thoughts recur in spoken word or other oral poetic forms. As humans, we return to those subjects that affect us, or that we consider important, and so, too, these letters return to the themes and topics that thread into the interwoven fabric of this work.

Given the nature of the writing and the subject matter, *Alphabet Soup* is not a quick or effortless read. I encourage you to take the time you need with the writing and absorb it at your own pace. In the end, this book will transport you to places you've previously been and to a few you'd never before contemplated, and this contemplation may then lead you on to fascinating and as-yet-unexplored terrain in your future.

AUTHOR'S NOTE

Alphabet Soup is conceptual, experimental, exploratory, emotional, and multifaceted, but most of all my hope is that it resonates within the reader at a frequency that moves fruitfully through their consciousness.

A. Gregory Frankson
Pointe-aux-Roches, Ontario
August 2023

I.

Illumination: 1. An illuminating or being illuminated, specif., a) a lighting up; supplying of light b) clarification; explanation c) enlightenment; instruction d) decoration with lights e) decoration of initial letters, manuscripts, etc. with designs, colors, etc. 2. the intensity of light per unit of area 3. the designs, tracings, etc. used in decorating manuscripts 4. the lights used in decorating a city, etc.

In the beginning was you.

Every breath you've ever drawn was a preordained testament to what inevitably came next. Much happened before you showed up on the scene, all new and fresh and unknowing and innocent.

Your lungs formed a nexus.

There has always been an air of expectation about you. The collision of genetics, history, racism, and gender politics rests so deeply in your DNA, the hostility of the world around you has no hope of ever digging it out of your bones, your flesh, your psyche.

You knew you were a blackberry before you learned the world's bush.

Without a doubt I knew you would require protection. I gave you the first taste of it when I defensively slammed my open hand into your chest as your first Christmas gift. That this palm would make us face your potential may have gone unnoticed by others present, but without it your first headstand may have taken all your understanding away.

I held my hand there until I'd corrected the angle of your first pitch because the curve would have jarred you too fast, and it was too soon for you to knuckle under.

Only after I released your diaphragm was I once again ready to exhale.

You probably do not understand any of this, and it's likely you think I'm mumbling nonsense. What memory could you possibly have of the earliest moments on your path? I'd be shocked if you knew. I don't really want you to know.

These remembrances have mercifully passed through your mind, selectively permeable, as it's been trained to be.

I took a shining to you the first time I set eyes on you, all rumpled and wrinkly as a soaked bulldog. You took your sweet time showing up, and every possible intervention could not speed the delivery of your first-class message. My heart, surreptitiously stolen, was collected and dropped into your carrier post-haste. Unbeknownst to you, you've transported it dutifully ever since.

Your possession of my couriered concern failed to deliver to you what you needed during all these years. It failed to stamp out absenteeism and left you with the residue of one single letter:

I.

I.

I: Five letters short of "family" and eleven short of "father figure." Eight letters short of "influence" and nine letters short of "supportive."

Zero letters short of forging your own identity from the spaghetti-lattice tangle of your chromosomal threads. Zero letters short of thereafter owning your own destiny.

And zero inclination for you to acknowledge the true genesis of your ascendancy.

The strangest part is that, in all likelihood, that single letter weighs on you like an albatross, preventing full flight. Any good mail should be about the air, but the reality of connection-consuming fires doused in the liquidity of constant passing currents have left you earthbound. Any elements of synchronicity that once existed have been washed away. Your youthful feathers remain brown-black, dark and downy, transforming flight into a trickier situation than it would have been otherwise.

I can't be sure because the distance between fledgling and father was created by fanning the fabled phoenix. It is difficult for everyone involved to rehash the ash without polluting the path you must follow to find the sustenance to take you beyond the present. With you, Christmas strikes tyrannous and strong as a winged hand; I dip and trip and plummet into the trough of your dismissal. The flight from you to holiness is a week and a fortnight that has always left me weak without foresight, despite the brilliant beauty of a birth star to guide the way.

Three times I tried to bedazzle you. I first shared what meagre gold I had at my disposal, conveyed to you through the hands of others, but imperfect proportions and poor planning left me impoverished in your eyes. Then I attempted to gum over the cracks in the foundation of our link but, lacking the skill to inject sealant to mend our fissures, I was cursed to concretize my failure. Finally, I sought redemption in the passions I learned burned deep within you, attempted to connect you to my yearnings and find common ground. The only terrain we shared lay arid and consumed by past fires. Men wiser than me arrived at your side to escort you away from the desolation of my surroundings.

My effort lay swaddled in the funereal. I laid such folly to rest long ago.

Despite this background I remain proud of what you have achieved and accomplished. I know without a single doubt in my mind that the elevation you have attained was impossible without massive effort.

There has been at least some mail that found its way to your hands inculcated with the sweetest love story you will ever read. With the way time has passed, there can be no way to begrudge you the lessons you now have taken to heart. The beat of your blood paces the movement of muscles that also know what it means to fly. They glide most productively at speed across the ice upon which you found greater comfort than any landscape associated with my form, shrouded in shadow, cursed to wander without aim. It is not without irony that your truth finds greater stability on ice than in an earthen foundation.

A fallow field is no place to find the water of life.

The light I provided you was a spectacular implosion reflected by the mirrors of a shared tragic history. It emanated as illumination so breathtaking that the only sane response was to turn away from the brightness and refuse to (set yourself) alight with any of it for the journey. It was blinding to me. It was clarifying for you. After reflection you instinctively knew what was best for us both.

Your ash-filled lungs expel acrid vapour whenever you turn in my direction. The release speaks not to me but to the need to externalize the conflagration. In my world, the passage of your breath lands silently on tympanic membranes hopelessly out of tune. There is no music in the metronomic rhythm of time as it marches inexorably across my life-starved savannah.

All connection has been burned away. Where you were planted, something new has grown in its place. You naturally regenerated, and in the place where new foliage has sprouted there is no space for a weed to attach itself.

Even so, the origin of your seedling self blooms from a garden that cultivated our common lineage. My implosion still reflects wherever I cast a shadow, no matter the obscure number of generations that pass before or in the future. As a result, know that across all passage of time, when you burn brightest, I reside in that spark. The tiniest granule of hope will always smoulder within my soul, and not even the stealing of my last breath will be powerful enough to extinguish it.

The nexus your lungs provided pivoted me toward oblivion, but even such a calamity can be redirected farther along an object's trajectory by another set of forces. I was not fully made when you spun me around to inflame the grimiest corners of my uncleanliness. Flame purifies as well as destroys. From this nexus I have flown a long distance, and to you I am not so clear across the expanse. It may be surprising what can be discovered upon closer examination.

You were the beginning of the journey. But now I've travelled a distance about as far away from you as I needed to find you in the first place. That's a long way to go to expect to find things exactly as they were frozen in your psyche. In time, you may find a desire to leave the ice behind, light a flame, and peer closer.

With you, Christmas is always approaching. My greatest wish for a Yuletide gift remains the transplantation of a blackberry bush sprouting brilliantly where our joint garden once stood.

Perhaps then we can both allow ourselves to drink more deeply of the water of life. §

D.

Disappoint: 1. to fail to satisfy the hopes or expectations of; leave unsatisfied 2. to undo or frustrate (a plan, intention, etc.); balk; thwart

Combined with *I*, you are the face of my existence, the way the law sorts me into categories, the blood that pulses deep within my official being. You are my vital statistics laser-printed onto a wallet-sized plastic card and easily verified by the empowered to assist, enforce, imperil, or penalize as circumstances (are) dictate(d).

You embody the singular ability to transform the now to the past. Tense.

Life drips from the gash in the core of my trunk like teardrop from duct, clings as it runs down my encrusted exterior, bark tougher than the bite of winter wind rattling my appendages. My energy drops like mercury as sap oozes from me with vascular abandon. Meant to sustain my strain, it instead takes away, sweet surrender, salting away my sustenance slick on the surface of my stability. Though I remain firmly rooted, I can no longer take a stand for you.

When we are too young to know what copulation means, men meant to serve and protect instead insert and project. Peddle a feeling astonishingly commonplace, hear it rasp at calluses grown over broken and bleeding skins, an abrasive washboard roughly corrugated against the memory of melody until eventually chaos careens from the cacophony. It takes years. The calluses never forget the virgin tears.

This was not meant to be true at home yet there you were, constable on patrol, copping whatever you feel, I kid you not. I was bypassed as silent syntheses climbed scales stealthily beyond my protected innocence. Black beats and pulses produced rhythmic sounds that were faint enough to escape my somnolescent notice, discordant harmonies in gloomy minors, key compositions consummated on the other side of the wall from where my notes rested.

Every body in that place maintained a cone of silence — a childhood teepee I didn't realize housed me more securely than the entire succession of my teenage addresses. Not until much later did I have any understanding that snitches get stitches, and sharp tools had already left wounds that were still in need of healing. A home is a house for love, and more of it was being shared beyond my knowing than words would reveal.

At some point many moons removed from your orbit, a satellite of truth traversed the grand expanses of the void, hurling projectile bile onto my temporal surface at cosmic speed. It gored me like a Chicxulub meteor and threw up enough sulphuric rage to blot out the last vestige of sunlight in my soul. My mind broke like an electoral promise. Speech was stolen from me like innocence. I could not identify the pitiful mewling, but my third eye understood it had come forth unbidden from my own throat. Despondent, I gargled the shards of a shattered childhood. Blood flooded my Eustachian tubes and overwhelmed the balance of my world.

It all came tumbling down.

Arrested development, arrested Black bodies imprisoned behind bars of shame, held against their will, strip-searched and humiliated, standing through a steady progression of daily trials, unable to acquit themselves and too oppressed by the system to make a successful appeal for clemency.

A life sentence pronounced in violation of the natural laws upon the wrongly convicted. There is no possible jailbreak when those being corrected lack the facility.

A home is a house for love, and none of it was being shared with me in words that would reveal the truth. For that, I would need to travel many moons beyond any possible insight that I was capable of attaining under heaven. We are now too old to know what copulation means when men meant to serve and protect instead insert and project. The confusion of my own past, colliding at speed with the real past as it happened on the surface of my understanding of how I reached the present ignorant of my own family history, hits me like a Don King–promoted Tyson fist.

I reel at the real, a film shredded beyond repair, a spool in search of renewed tension to hold its story together.

I do not identify with any of it, at all. My capacity to carry the weight you've burdened me with has torn at my old calluses, abrading them until they break open red and raw. Everything you've ever said drowns, overwhelmed in the blood surging through my ear canals. My compassion flatlines like a pulse under attack by cardiac arrest. Defibrillation of fibs flubs and the shocking effect instills stillness in my heart. It has gone cold to you, never to be resuscitated, beyond reanimation. §

Y.

Yearning: deep or anxious longing, desire, etc.

It has been said many times in many places that the third time is the charm.

We met in the sky, boosted aloft on unstable stilts, standing amongst those charmed to live in elevated places. We combined, a brew of star-bright suns luminous as light shimmer surface of seaway bored its way into safe harbour. A third ingredient mixed in with us to complete the alchemy —

delicious flavour to be deciphered through mélange of melodic rhythmic patter freestyled from the belly of the petri dish. We were collective curiosities under the microscope, a chemical mix of biologicals at the centre of a cauldron.

You were the vanilla to my chocolate to his caramel, an unexpected amalgam of colour, providing flavour to an otherwise bland blend of the bumptious offspring of the beer-addled maple-dropped bourgeoisie in the belly of the brouhaha.

We dropped lines more skillfully than those kids could ever hope to snort them.

They got high as we gave them all the vapours
Rapped the insides of minds pulling off lyrical
  capers
Disseminated knowledge that burned like
  Zippo'ed papers
Intoxicated with talent for these privileged
  escapers …

As a trio, we worked with the raw material of verb and adjective and braggadocio in ebbs and flows that made the St. Lawrence envious. We hurled our artistry from the top levels of our conscious surroundings into the *fleuve* below.

What can you do with a drunken sailor early in the morning, come from below decks to bedazzle the crew? Never had I felt as adrift amongst the iciest of icebergs masquerading as starch-collared penguins patrolling the wrong hemisphere. We tied one on while tides turned. By the time we'd melted enough to raise sea levels by an inch or two, we'd set off for safety and left the rest as stranded emperors on ice floes.

We've voyaged forward strangely syncopated in our battering by the jet stream of success ever since.

We can take the three letters that were first slurped from this alphabet soup and mix them into self-sufficiency. Do it. Yourself. See where it can take you; once you arrive on the precipice of the monumental, be sure to look behind. Yourself. Do it. Inevitably there I will be: Just as it was when you debated where to take yourself and landed on a capital thought. Just as it was when you sucked all the capital from it ponderously and changed over to light up the big smoke. Weaving through the backwash navigated in the wake of privileged contemporaries, I don windbreaker and wet wellies to weather maritime storms as if I were born to it. As you were.

Those beer hall scofflaws joined parties that throw everything but the kitchen sink at people instead of sinking into the song of kitchen parties thrown to join people with beer. Your parties always seemed like greater fun, so when I found my way to the capital it felt a more natural place to distill my distemper by placing an order for a tune. Drummed up it was, from the first, by instruments of ambition and striving. Object of desire always within reach, though never meant to be held for very long. We shared mutual appreciation for the chase, and mutual regard for each other's inability to hold fast once furtive grasping found purchase. Class struggle is real. In retrospect, it is doubtlessly appropriate that we should both have to struggle. With class.

Y?

Yes, Y. A slanted letter, and you cannot make it straight.

It's as if the world cannot hear the voices of the talented without amplification by the powerful. As a speaker I wish to be heard from every mount — royal in stature — and from every towering piece piped cacophonous, never flagging, a cannonading explosion of creative armaments from the harbour of my mind, riding an aural tsunami that inundates every citizen in every constituency.

Everywhere I went, there you were — creating space in creative spaces, absorbing, expanding, always seeking to be the reason the room felt full. We became friends fast as the buttons that cinched together the shirts you didn't need to give me from your back. It was unnecessary, for most times it already adorned mine. In chemise I shimmied to the sounds of multi-instrumentation shared on loop, prepared with lip, pick, stick, string, and fingertips plugging holes in skillful succession, preventing levity from draining downward into sorrows. Your group fiddled as we burned through bottles of liquid courage, each lick encouraged by the previous, bouncing bodies on barnwood floors, exulting, catapulted skyward by ecstasy in foot-high bursts, repeated and repeated and repeated in three-part harmony. Privateers and merchant marine raised glasses to your bodhrán-bodacious ballads and jingles, filling sporrans and bellies alike, enriching the world like buriers of bounty in backwoods backyards, beyond the visioning of mere mortals.

We plotted and planned like eleven oceans ready to overrun the earth. For us, the best laid plans set us off in a north-north-easterly direction, banded together tightly, my voice echoing yours in harmonic resolution. Brotherhood overcame every disappointment, any unrequited love of the art, of the heart, of the sullen slings and arrows life could impart — you wore your armour and each projectile that struck it only served to make it sing more melodically in the reverberation. Survival became your chorus, resilience your verses, determined forward movement your *D.S. al Coda* — all looped back in service of the grand ambition for yet another strike of chords and flight of cords. Your dedication to the battle reinforced my own desire to reach out for more and insinuate myself into ever more spaces that artfully dodge my efforts at acceptance.

Ever yearning for the life those who were charmed to be born into elevated spaces took for granted even as they showed us how unworthy they were of their ill-gotten fortune.

Miss fortune, when she comes knocking, and the rich sound clash that filled the empty room will forever haunt your dreams.

Instead, we choose to raise our voices higher than our stations to tune out the static. We home in on the frequencies that project our passions most clearly, finding the songs that speak of our souls and setting them to the task of kicking down doors. We've co-written more than just musical magic. We are co-authors of our own demises, our own surprises, our fiendishly delicious table-settings, our relentlessly reimagined pathways to a proclivity for productivity.

Every time we've chosen to innovate a new passageway through the problems, or partnership to overachieve in the face of rumoured defeat, we've somehow managed to come through the other side as if reborn. Push too hard and rupture; refuse to push and get stuck. Find balance. Expend energies as if your sacks of gold depend on it — don't go out like that, man. Behave as if bailout is only meant for sinking ships and you're a lifelong landlubber. Drag the boat ashore and pull a tarp over it. Preserve it for future forays. I may not choose to enter the waters with you, but I will chart a course. This will com(e to)pass at the moment you need assistance with a new direction. I will always be prepared to rise to your aid like tides of the Atlantic near the source of your life spring.

Could you have conceived in your wildest imagining the expansive panoramas we'd traverse together?

Yet of course certain straits were destined for solo navigation, places we sailed into on our own, salty splashes against hull as dire groans and ominous splintering of assaultive rock ground progress to a halt. We could do nothing to prevent each other's occasional shipwrecks, the crack of splitting hulls loud as siren songs luring the unwary into foolish foundering. Once immobilized in the wake of disaster usually caused by the false seduction of illusion, manatee-like in the mists amidst the missed middle of set course, there is nothing left for the witness except cruise at the vanguard of rescue.

We have protection programmed into our ties that bind. Remove one now and tie it to the tugboat, let it spring from ensnarement and guide you to a pier, accepting of damage and equipped to repair. Set sail once again once reconstitution completed — find new current back to see and appear accepting of future ensnarement, to repair equipped for the accepting of damage that may come from ties that bind to another guide sure to appear in the middle amidst a missed set course through the mists.

Survival becomes chorus, resilience the verses, determined forward movement a *D.S. al Coda* — all looped back in service of grand ambitions for yet another strike of chords and flight of cords. This time, know how to keep moving past previous markers, forward progress demands current inattention to the pullback, lest the composition be ruined by too much repetition — amplified dedication to the score, read the lines, feel the silences in rests and resonance in *crescendo*, march on at *allegro*, and embrace the *pianissimo* when it demands restraint in soft moments. Ride the waves astride clipper-like rapid release of verb and adjective and braggadocio in ebbs and flows that propel us with (astro)nautical force toward the next elevation in our lifelong explorations. The quest continues with gale at our backs.

Tell me — when we hurled our artistry from the top levels of our conscious surroundings into the *fleuve* below the room where we first joined forces, could you foresee the campaign ahead? Did you suspect that we'd somehow find ourselves ensnared longer than Americans in Afghanistan, just as poorly resolved, yet still somehow filled with desire to break through the battlements meant to deny us a birthright with which we both still lacked acquaintance?

Where we combined, a brew of star-bright suns luminous as light shimmer surface of seaway bored its way into safe harbour. We may have been in that port on that portentous night, but we'd visit many more — to fight our way ashore, or to be accepted into the warm embrace of the expectant, or even to be greeted by wary furrowed brows on the envious and malevolent. Every time, we'd find ourselves questing anew for a stable anchorage.

Though we have never been sojourners satisfied with such a station for too long.

All these years later, we still voyage forward strangely syncopated in our battering by the jet stream of success. And remain sternly unbowed.

Out on the swell, one couldn't ask for a better shipmate. §

R.

Respect: 1. a feeling of high regard, honor, or esteem: to have respect for a great artist 2. the state or condition of being held in honor or esteem: to have the respect of one's sons 3. deference or dutiful regard: respect for the law 4. consideration; courteous regard: to have respect for the feelings of others 5. [pl.] courteous expressions of regard: now chiefly in pay one's respects, to show polite regard by visiting or presenting oneself 6. a particular point or detail: right in every respect 7. reference; relation: with respect to the problem

1.

Tell me what it has been like on the other side, veiled from view, eternally untouched by terrestrial testing, spectres beyond inquisition, spectators beyond watching.

I do not even remember how to approach you anymore.

There was only one way for my family to do it before: long red ribbons tied across a big smoke under temperate sky, fuelled by the glare of a red rocket's mechanized eye, lamps to see our way west. I was a young man, perhaps too young to claim the title of man, an isle of robbed youth. Life moved fast — so quickly that in the hearts and bodies of some of my compatriots it barely had time to claim citizenship before asylum turned to inter(n)ment to a one-way trip across the veil. Somehow in my stumbling, I avoided the grasp reaping sown seeds planted in blackness. With so little light, it's amazing how any managed to sprout.

Snapped from reverie to exchange one red ribbon for another, mapped out cross-stitching of nearly impoverished fabrics socially cohered from there from here, I allowed myself to be guided down rear steps to ground level, bust from gut of asphalt-guided wagon to perch on paved platforms. Walked alongside. Flowed with mass at volume, high density of barely not poor and nearly broke that babbled into underground caverns. Emergence sees means of movement meet the many at three- to five-minute intervals, in transit gents with command of conveyance, whistles in mouths, referees of our mobility.

Two blasts, and we take flight to find a finch at north end of rail ribbon, departed from Eglinton in the city of Eggleton, conveyance of ancient carriage elevated to modern art form. Long stretches with short stops at midsection of run from home to lands fouled by the (un)fair who've learned to live on steals and wild pitches while avoiding double plays.

It was upon such base paths that I would eventually arrive safe, running through to ensure I'd find you there in that place with a smile on your face upon greeting mine. I can barely find you now in my mind's eye, shimmering spectre, the completeness of your features nearly washed away by the decades. Despite the difficulty of re-rendering your presence in its fullness seated at my side, the banquet of your love has never ended for me. Your eternally childlike grin lights up my remembrances like a freshly illuminated hall in the newest moments before it was prepped for the feasting. You will not, cannot, have never, will not ever, age.

I must pause. Tear blinks. We were so young. Deep breaths.

• • •

No matter how many times I was brought to spend time with you, I could not relate to your home of three brothers. Two youngers too young to tow, so we left them at dockside as we roamed, twinned spirits, best of friends, subconsciously linked with eyes only for the stars. When they hollered for telescopic engagement, we rendered them out of focus, preoccupied with our own explorations. Sojourners with truth on our tongues, wind in our sails, and each other's arms linked, we had become brothers of a different sort. Never again would I experience such effortless male connection with one so like me, who so liked me, who knew me to the molecular level — words were substandard energy we subjugated to crackling pulse of our unspoken kinetic kinship. We were more than friends, more than brothers, more than mere boys at play on a disrespected dead-end drive evocative of a nautical gem at the tip of the Bruce Peninsula.

Inevitably, our explorations were always ended by maternal orders we were far too young to countermand. Grudging return to shelter resulted in a well-nourished memory to be stowed away for later examination as I reverse retraced red ribbons and rocketed red-eyed in mechanical fashion, guided by lamps to see our way back east across a big smoke under a nearly sunset sky.

We never wished to be separated physically but I could always feel you, as if with shoulders conjoined, the warmth of you always present and support mutually assured. Despite the distances and difficulties of daily dialogue, you spoke between my ears ephemerally and I minded not. Tied to you by a heartstring in a way I could not fully comprehend, for we were not socialized as boys to be attuned to such transcendental twanged tones — at least not while both organs shared the same resonance. I would learn, painfully, to lament and long for its sound once one went to ground. The reverberations still thrum faintly, a vibration destined never to find full arrest.

In a time before we could dial smartly beyond rotary and coiled cable to retain ongoing connection through electric ribbons in the sky, I could only wonder during the in-between times about what you and your brothers did on your quotidian quests. The community connection of our life-givers that preceded our births and bonded us like blood family was rooted in the tropical soil of our ancestral provenance, then relocated, rediscovered, and reforged in snow and ice, eventually to be granted to us as the most precious of gifts. We carried it forward under their watchful and approving eyes, joyous in our jaunts when our forces joined like preternaturally irresistible magnetic attraction. From opposite sides of the city, we remained perpetually drawn to each other, constantly in search of assistance we needed for us to gaze upon each other in person, like the closing loop of a red ribbon knotting the fabric together for strength.

It was during one of those in-between times on a quotidian quest when you left me dockside for a telescopic engagement that rendered me out of focus, preoccupied with your own explorations with one of your two too-young younger brothers. The curiosity of youth overpowered all caution as you and your friends cut through creek valley on the climb back to Tobermory, a shortcut that would cut you short in a fashion cold as the harshest of winter's depths. On the day before heartstrings were set to strumming by lovebirds in song across the full surface of the turtle's back, you dipped a toe into a mildly fuelled fulmination of nature's temperate sunlit power. One false step along the muddy Yorkish shoreline of waterway caused you to give way. As friends gasped, you grasped for reeds to grant you a moment to read the perils of your position, battered by the overflow of mid-February early onset of spring conditions. If only you could have sprung from the fresh(water) trap in which you'd been ensnared, then younger brother would not have rushed forward and attempted to release you from it with his own bare hands. He was no match for the power of the stream. It snuffed his flame of adrenaline with tragic ease, yanked a response too overwhelming for him to physically counteract, and swept both of you deep into its entangling fury.

My lifelong fear of rushing water came naturally and at a young age.

They could not find you through their collective eyes for three days after you had become shimmering spectre, the completeness of your vivified features washed away by the passage of tumultuous spring runoff. Your spirit relocated long before rediscovery of your form, reforged lifeless by melted snow and ice, taking from us the most precious of gifts. The grief compounded by simultaneous discovery of fraternal frame beached nearby, infuriatingly expired long in advance of his best before date, blue as the ice, damp as snow, fully melted away. Your worlds went black in a creek as Black as us and as bleak as our presupposed prospects.

My household knew nothing of this until tube buzzed with ribboned lines flowing across its screen, where depicted anchor dropped a lead weight onto my entire being later that evening. At the top of the hour when they confirmed your final hour had transpired, I drowned my sorrows in wretched, uncontrollable sobs. Our ribbon irreparably torn, your middle brother eternally a hero, your youngest brother as sick for you as he was sick with fever that day, your family resigned to return you to the tropical soil of our ancestral provenance. We were both barely two digits in age and yet one of us had to be left behind with a permanent one at the front of our numbered years. When I look back, more than three decades later, I still search fervently for you in my mind's eye.

But there you are and have remained all this time, with your brother, on the other side, veiled from view, eternally untouched by terrestrial testing, spectres beyond inquisition, spectators beyond watching.

I have forgotten how to approach you and cannot find you anymore.

• • •

Regret: 1. a troubled feeling or remorse over something that has happened, esp. over something that one has done or left undone 2. sorrow over a person or thing gone, lost, etc. 3. [pl.] a response declining an invitation: he sent his regrets before the deadline.

2.

Your ashes reside as deeply in my flesh as in the hills of Xaymaca, an essential part of my make-up, your memory made flesh in me and your story unsilenced through these printed paragraphs of personal testimony. I bury part of you here so that your soul can continue to live — for as long as these pages can be found, so, too, can you and your brother be discovered and remembered.

The only grace saved in your untimely departure is that you did not die in vain, for each time I walk a path beside a Big Smoke waterway I see physical manifestation of both of your memories. Equipment meant for the saving of life stand as monuments to your sacrifice, and each time I come across these totems to your tragedy I stop, rest a hand on the post supporting ring and hook, and fervently search through prayer for the loop of a red ribbon that once knotted our fabric together for strength. I take the moment to think of the large, framed photos of three brothers in a home that now only accommodates one, a posthumous medal of bravery gracing the central frame, the eyes of the brother to the left shining with the life I knew so well.

Prayer concluded, I pat the ring, look to the water, and continue my journey, shoulder burning with the remembrance of scarring severance of conjunction. §

J.

Jealous: 1. very watchful or careful in guarding or keeping: jealous of one's rights 2. a) resentfully suspicious of a rival or a rival's influence: a husband jealous of other men b) resentfully envious c) resulting from such feelings: a jealous rage 3. ARCHAIC requiring exclusive loyalty: "for I the Lord your God am a jealous God"

I often wondered, before words knew how to insistently generate themselves on my tongue for powerful purposes, why you used yours to lacerate my innocent form. Both word and tongue were beasts burdening my barely birthed cognition with your lashings of overwhelming scorn. Initially, you approached me like a cat burglar, desperately trying every method available to snuff out my light. I stubbornly refused to be extinguished — either by extended dips underwater, or the flow of startled vehicular traffic, or by bleeding out onto a rugged rusty-coloured runner. I did not comprehend your nightly prayers for full cessation of my animation, though I instinctively understood it was the only way I could to please you completely.

Over time, I grew accustomed to your clanging tin-pot kitchen dictations and bullying breakfast beatdowns. Once able to take the heat and keep on cooking, you changed the recipe with the wickedness of Scotch bonnet secreted into Irish stew. My mutinying mouth never stood a chance with you. It did not take you long to turnkey demands into crushing consequences. Circumstances set you on a course of corrections. If you were to be charged with monitoring a delinquent juvenile, you sought to be absolutely certain that in that cage your word was law.

No one ever asked you what you wanted so you turned sentinel keeper of your own counsel. The elders in your circle insisted you grasp the import of the moment in the interest of enlightenment. Your fingers failed to lift, spurring elevated rage to burn like a torch you refused to carry. Did you feel infantilized at your every attempt to ignite a flame? All you wanted in those days was to be in command of your own domain. While care for me was burdensome for others, your choice to spurn overbearing burning imperatives made you maverick in maven's clothing.

You've been on fire ever since.

You radiate passion like a kerosene lantern guiding you onto a path of self-made freedom. Each step becomes firmer with your growing self-assurance. You made a break for it even when the world told you survival on your own wasn't possible. It's needless to prepare yourself for a premature grave when the blaze inside your soul gives you so much life. My eyes upon you turned teary from staring at your firecracker brilliance. It was time for you to defy the dark in service of your spark, wholly on your own terms.

J.

Your mind smoulders with the intensity of volcanic rock stoked by geothermal expulsions blasted through crackled crust. Magma memory of what you've continuously created flows thick as liquefied perseverance — reshaping your world with your every pressure-provoked eruption. As always, you cannot be contained nor restrained. Every downward slope that conveyed you into depths has precipitated the beginning of a new cycle. It's incredible to watch you scorch earth to revitalize the land and prepare it for new growth. No matter where you are or where you seek to move to next, your slash-and-burn tendencies always, in the end, manage to amply feed the ones you love.

You proved that there is life and opportunity at the bottom of every valley.

As my toddler terror transformed to adult awe of your terraforming endurance, I could only marvel at the way you formulated your victory. Despite the ongoing threat of a molten meltdown, those you brought into the world you created quickly learned to till the dirt and reap the harvest. It was only possible because fields formed from your heated redevelopment provided a fertile bounty infused into the soil. At some point I wished to see you find new flame to transform brush fire to bonfire to five-alarm blaze.

One by one, your four most prized creations sought out their own new pastures, fortified by the life-augmenting nourishment from your plots, capable of self-sustenance due to lessons taught by your wise cultivations. Their departures provided you the space to reshape surroundings once more to fit the evolved needs of a firebrand. To reorient your terrain to fully accommodate a new hand, you chose to construct a bailey as the first step to building the castle of your dreams. Each brick is a volcanic tribute to your youthful defiance, every coating of binding mortar an acknowledgement of your bravery and strength.

One day I hope to be so fortunate as to find myself set ablaze with comparable fire. §

Z.

Zealous: full of, characterized by, or showing zeal; ardently devoted to a purpose; fervent; enthusiastic

You were like a flower at its fullest bloom that evoked maximum delight at the peak of its blossoming. Like an awakened trillium, we wove patterns in clusters of threes, seed planted in the third year of a new century, bearing the sweet redolence of endless possibility. Your cells, wedged at the base of an edifice of concrete and brick, were a flat of chambers laid out in orderly sweetness. You tended them in concert with other worker bee companions, building a basis for bounty with youthful diligence.

Within those honeycomb walls, I droned on about my appetites, dreams, and aspirations, feeling as if my head grew larger with each inane exhalation. You spoke of previous frolics in fields of wild roses before seeking out new learning opportunities through a Mecca-like eastern pilgrimage. Somehow, by good fortune our minds met in the middle, and we made merry with the meagre means at our fingertips. We were learning to find our ways in the world as you interned intently, and I came to terms with new realities in a garden foreign to us both. We knew from the start that our intersecting flight patterns within such floral surroundings were fleeting.

That spring and summer brought sustained sunshine to both our lives, feeding photosynthesis to produce remembrances propelled by the energies of our youth. No deep thinking about what the autumn may bring. We stayed present to germinate the gift. When seasons changed, your pilgrimage pulled you east to habituate in the valley of a saint, to stroll cobblestones that bordered where you could see well beyond the present into a new future for yourself. As you flew off to new meadows, fervent in fidelity to the expansion of your ambitions, I settled into new patterns of flight, on my own once again. In defiance of distance, we retained desire to remain in contact. Your stinging dives into cycles of blue-flag pollinations did not prevent friendship from springing into our existences.

I cobbled together a creative composition to share with language lovers mounted royally astride snowy one-way drag ways. After a lyrical night of alluring aurality in a madly poetic milieu, we flitted into a flight of friendly familiarity, once again on perpendicular paths, even more briefly than ever before. Though we tried to keep it light as always, I felt its weight a bit more keenly this time as you zipped your way aloft and away.

Z.

Months turned into years as your flight pattern found elevation — lofty heights at which you fastened your wings onto your prayers. New appeal to higher powers brought your life repeated blessings. Your golden-hued zigzag Zen betrayed the rapidity of raises typical of a well-earned climb. While your formidable persistence set you to soaring above mountains, I remained in the valleys, ground-level scavenger, performing no true service for the hive in my frantic search for sustained sustenance, stranded, famished, and cold. Starving for succour, the course of my streams of conscious de- and re-coupling bent and twisted within the fluvial trough like the spilled spaghetti of a troublesome toddler. The tangle of under-fulfilled dreams cluttered my mind while you found your stride at the foothills of good fortune. I cheered for you from afar, even as I stood sauce-splattered and creatively malnourished.

Despite my discontentment, I fortuitously found myself rostered for a road trip through mountains I'd never seen before to translate words spoken into messages of youthful hope. I climbed every mountain, entrapped by their beauty, greeting each morning with a strong and white gaze upon an elevated snow-capped world. When it was me versus the inclines, my automatic response geared me down with hopes and prayers that I could summit up with the tip of my tongue.

I spoke whirlwinds at each stop along the way until I paused to revel, stoked. A detour had come to pass, and I took it to find two sisters — Alberta and Louise. They bade me take an evening and a night (in)to (a) park where, third time around, it felt as if perpendicularity yielded to decampment in a mere blink of a moment. I knew the years had been kind as I watched you levitate to leave, buzzing brightly skyward with unceasing forward energy. It was clear your unflagging attention to organic growth had spurred your flourishing as predictably as filtered sunlight in a well-tended greenhouse.

And then it was time for you to harvest the sweetness.

Z.

At your zenith, you have become the queen of your own hive, bustling with industry, productive and regal. Without you the rest of us literally meet our own ends, starved of pollinating care that feeds our ability to exist. Throughout our occasionally intersecting paths we have flown into our futures, supportive of the buzz each has generated along the way, independently certain that more honey to sate our souls shall surely flow soon. At the head of your colony, you urge your workers to unceasingly preserve growth and survival — a communicative dance trumpeting control and competence.

Boosted by the zip of the zephyr, ascending above the earth, we each gained increases in altitude from which to coax and coach ourselves to even greater heights. Twinned timetables we kept when our flight patterns first zigged and intersected have long since diverged, your beeline zag zipping you onto a course that later yielded twins fraternal and familiar to your flesh. Through them the purpose of heartfelt commune will allow you to live forever in the cells of honeycombs to come.

At the end of the alphabet, you hold the power of termination. You've become a new beginning to deny an abrupt end to your line, a reversal of terminus that transcends time. And as you rest at the head of your nest, it is as clear as cloudless skies:

Your prosperity is assured because, like queens everywhere, you have the royal jelly. §

Q.

Quarrel: 1. a cause for dispute 2. a dispute or disagreement, esp. one marked by anger and deep resentment 3. a falling out; breaking up of friendly relations

The look on your face said it all.

Eyes with an onyx stare as hard as diamonds, mouth set beyond match, face with an expression that wasn't playing games. Stance set with balled fists on hips, thighs astride the world with feet rooted, body as immovable as a mountain. Once the flash of annoyance twisted your countenance towards anger, there was no way to come down from the peak except on the crest of a life-threatening snowslide. Words that cut sharp as obsidian blades unleashed in ritual fury battered my bluster without mercy.

And because I was me and you were you, there was no escaping the avalanche.

There was never any point in quibbling or squabbling — in this trivia challenge, every utterance I issued was the wrong answer. Your determined verbal battering stumped me and left me breathless. I understood early what it meant to be utterly defenceless.

You have the vexation buried so deeply in you it cannot be excavated — no archaeological excursion could ever dig what you've hidden away from prying eyes. It's so far gone you don't even know it's there, but I see it rise up like the undead in a zombie flick, coming for me as I run as fast as tiny legs can carry me. Finding a strategy to short-circuit the intensifying electrical storm threatening to end me was a feast for the brain. Light work for you didn't elevate my self-esteem, yet somehow my admiration for you never diminished.

This could only be true because there was far more clarity of vision than destructive power surge generated by your incandescence. Your smile was a 1980s playground filled with early childhood delights. Being under your watchful gaze was like a living under a spotlight that kisses so precisely that only your best features are illuminated. The magnification of everything magnificent about you, your lineage, and your dreams for us, brought our most delicate features into sharp relief.

More than once I have wondered what your eyes have seen. What did it look like to drink in the salty expanses of transatlantic wavelengths on one of the passages our forebears were never blessed enough to take? Could you see sharks lurking below the surface of our tribal traumas as swells crashed against hulls as relentlessly as wayward whips on exposed ebony? When the outline of the island homeland of our former oppressors lifted lazily from the distant horizon, did you fear setting foot on their manicured gardens or long to inch back towards your adolescent *yahd*?

Took more than an ounce of strength to pound your way through the currency of an overtaxed situation to reap the dividends of your life-altering investment. Your interest in raising kings and queens while resisting pawns with violent checkered pasts remains a testament to strategic brilliance. Knowing the price of a compounded growth strategy is diligent dedication to a stay-the-course mindset in the face of potential future folly only causes me to marvel more at your prescience. It was as if you could see the generations to come and you chose to meet them on the only terrain where they stood a chance to take a stand.

To get to them before they could arrive, you escaped the bile in an organ that traversed a gigantic pool at Her Majesty's behest. Departure was a liberation across leagues of litres littered with the lamentations of a people uneasy with the sway of hulls. The courage to consider the crossing of graveyard ingratitude in search of solace shocks the heart. In a land whiter than plantation foremen, accessed after dancing through straits of icebergs to beat winter freeze-up, you sought stability. I am not sure I could ever have been resilient enough to uproot twice in search of greener pastures.

Especially when I think of first port at a foreign dock on an ice-choked river.

Our lineage confronted the first solitude on a snow-packed dock unprepared for the wetness and cold. Upon physical confrontation, tropical persistence crumbled as it succumbed to flakes of wrath piled high at the point of contact. Properly chastened, a hasty retreat beaten after an initial frosty frolic emblazoned consequences for unbundled burdens unforgettably into our psyches for decades. Each of us has chosen their own way to deal with cyclically short days and cold nights. You never forgot why your blood pumps heated through your veins. You found ways to recharge your cells in lands reminiscent of the home from which we were pruned but where the original bush continues to grow wild in the hills.

Once rails were ridden and second solitudes recognized, clippings were reset in hopes that they would take eagerly to the new soil. Throughout the years to follow, the branches found new footing and forms of prosperity, springing forth with new growth in fits and starts. Few branches withered as the health of the whole took hold. There was not always enough sun or water but never too much love in tending to the needs of the planted. Eventually, there comes a point when the new bush grows strong enough to reproduce its health in new fields. When its seeds sprout in new places it is a tribute to ancestral hands that planted them. Nearly three dozen successful seedings sends a powerful message.

Our seeds started in an unmanicured *yahd* and yet you managed to birth a garden filled with beauty. You are the nourishment of our ambitions, the placeholder that permitted our seeds to spread and multiply. There's no argument that without you, we would be scattered to the winds. With you, our foundation in a land not familiar to us became our familial inheritance.

We now find ourselves rooted where we cannot be torn out of the ground we occupy. We got here by braving the expanses of sea that stole much of our humanity. You emerged triumphant and celebrated by living well. The best revenge against oppression is building an indestructible legacy.

And I see it all when your onyx eyes flash in my mind, hard as diamonds. Precious treasure. §

U.

Uncertain: 1. not surely or certainly known; questionable; problematic 2. not sure or certain in knowledge; doubtful 3. not definite or determined; vague 4. liable to vary or change; not dependable or reliable 5. not steady or constant; varying

Carried on airborne conveyance and taken flight from foreign fields, you landed wheels down and eyes wide open. It's not like the journey was your choice — an escape plan iterated into itinerary had the initial impact of a withdrawal from where you felt safe, akin to kidnapping. You were both part of the baggage, hastily packed, your inner order an afterthought, hoping the contents necessary for the trip made it in before being zippered shut. Ever since, you've been searching to see if everything ever got fully unloaded. Not certain that it did.

One of you the size of a personal item; the other the size of a carry-on. Both forced thereafter to carry on as if you'd never crossed a plain blue sky to find new abode. Words spoken in hushed tones accentuated the disconnect. A mash-up served with pidgin peas and rice underneath the spice hesitantly left behind. Who made a meal of the first attempt to find a morsel to satisfy your palates? Who curried favour with those who framed you as jerks and left you with a rancid taste in your mouths? How did you find solace when solitary in a soulless space?

Piling into a taxi after taxiing, your crew disembarked after fleeing third-class carriage to assume nothing in coveted first-class conveyance. Windows, doors, steering, brakes, locks, newfound freedom — power everything. You stared through the pane as the world whipped by, the windshield offering inadequate protection from the inversion of your comprehension. Everything felt like it was on the wrong side and suddenly what was left behind seemed right. Disorientation flooded your vision even as excitement tipped you out of balance. The need for steadying influence was too apparent in that moment. You looked to find their stability as you rocked to the new rhythms imposed by the lay of this new land. The drive ended when the fare was paid. One hopes the charge was fair for the journey travelled to find what you could now consider to be home.

Your first tentative steps upon the dirt of a new land stained your trainers with Laurentian mud. As a result, before you ever got to experience anything, your entrance was already sullied. Wiping your feet clean at the threshold would mean transferring the filth of the owner's yard onto their own welcome mat, and you felt sure that would be discourteous. How many exhausted one-way sojourners had similar thoughts when they arrived at the doorstep of a new life? Left no choice but to follow your ancestors into the future of the now, you entered and prepared for the best. A couple of sneakers with new challenges afoot.

U.

Finding out where your jigsaw-jagged edges helped to complete the bigger picture was the first major puzzle. It felt like every time you found your fit, your colour was wrong, accented by several elements of inconsistency with the neighbours, clearly out of place. The shape of your yearning for acceptance was never quite adequate.

Chafing from the friction when you ran up against others, you decided to morph and mould into a new shape, while still young and malleable, rather than become frozen stiff, inflamed to brittle fragility. With corners rounded and edges smoothed, boundaries reconstituted to pass the test of complementarity, core material completely unaltered, and difference less accented, you found a place on the edge of the frame: Not central to the composition and barely integral enough to help the whole make sense. But at this stage of the game, inclusion was all that mattered.

Into a bubbling cauldron you were thrown like a stewing bone — breaking through superficial surface to add flavour to the raging brew below. The complex blend of ingredients would take as many generations to unravel as it took for them to merge so unpleasantly. The tragedy is that such an inheritance sickened people who ladled it unsuspectingly into their mouths in search of nutrition. Seeing which hand could stir the pot most vigorously became a campaign of attrition. You were caught up in the soup, unable to alter it, determined not to drink it, bound by duty to take the cup offered up by sturdy hands. When you gulped it down, the taste of over-seasoned inheritance scorched your insides. Intergenerational trauma.

Instead, you found ways to retain your place in the larger puzzle and pursue passions that placed you at the centre of the story. You nursed ambitions that sounded like they were produced to move crowds. They came to complement the space taken up by your midnight dreams and daytime fantasies. When people see you in the middle of the broader narrative, bringing a new complexion, demanding to be observed by the willfully oblivious — only then will they realize that who you are at your core has never changed or been lost.

Now, instead of worrying about the stains of the past, you resolve to leave indelible footsteps in the present to guide others in the future. One person's dirt and filth are another's ink to stamp a story of resilience into the land that preserves the pace of your passage.

After I am no more and it is time for me to fly away, there is comfort in knowing that you will still be able to see the way forward. And that your care in messing up the owner's welcome mat with their own mud helps others find their way. Not everything that you'd meant to carry with you overseas may have made it to your destination, but the critical items were passed along.

And what of the baggage that still threatens to weigh you down as you attempt liftoff into a clear blue sky? §

V.

Vindictive: 1. revengeful in spirit; inclined to seek vengeance 2. said or done in revenge; characterized by vengeance: vindictive punishment

1.

Such a deceptive letter — accommodating and open at the top with a bottom tip sharp as a venomed fang. Since coming to full knowledge about the poisons you carry for deadly effect, I've learned to treat you with respect. You do not frighten me as much as provide me with a lesson in how to scout the bushes for wild dangers before breaking trail. It has stuck with me every time I've gone to take a hike ever since.

The beginning was innocuous enough. A casual contact between mutual friends was the first time our paths crossed. No explosions lit up the skies in a festival of fire like past pyrotechnic symphonies on Ontario shores. Initial interactions that were loose as laces on a kindergartner first tripped us up. You fastened shoelaces, graduated to new roles and places; I remained, focused pupil, with untied laces.

You changed your status, danced to a different tune; you stayed on the sidelines while your techniques helped others to find their feet. For whatever reason, we continued to dance round one another like sweet science shadows. One particular club for cool kids was the place where our steps became confident as a primary schooler with excellent shoelace technique. Dangling laces became knots and loops finished the action while your strings' pressure held my tongue fast. Any objections I should have spoken were silenced, and we were off at a foxtrot.

We swayed cheek to cheek, dancing in rhythm to the strains of sound judgments, trying not to mash each other's toes. Neither of us knew how much the other was improvising. Our feet found nothing but floor after each cycle as weeks became months became years.

The missteps, once they began, were all mine, scuffing your footwear's white leather with my dark, marking sole. My discombobulated choreography left a permanent tarnish. Our steps slowly devolved into a listless disharmony of left feet and your extremities became increasingly rigid with each number. I should have suspected that you were more aware of both of our tendencies than you initially let on. Against the best of my instincts, we continued to move fatefully through our patterns one tune after another.

By the time our dancing brought new life to our situation, we were a pair of sullied sole-mates in need of fresh apparel. We knew, if we were honest with each other, that it was time to find new dance partners, but there was no honesty to be found between emotional wallflowers.

2.

To nurture the spark we ignited, we journeyed blindly into the underbrush, stumbling, searching for fuel before it twinkled into nothingness. When we found a suitable spot, we dug a pit and fed it logs and oxygen until it expanded into a roaring fire. I, not being much of a woodsman, and you, not being any sort of passionate camper, made it work somehow. At least, at the beginning.

Since we found ourselves in the forest, we went through the motions of roughing it. Hacking away at (our) nature(s) and hunting for necessary sources of subsistence, we gathered an abundance of random sweetness harvested along the path. It helped make our craven creations somewhat palatable.

Back at the campsite, where we drove tent pole deep into shifting sands for tenuous anchorage, there could be no security in the shelter we erected beneath the trees. The necessities of life required to satisfy Maslow were meant, in your mind, to establish and maintain a base hierarchy through games that left me famished, odds ever in your favour. I didn't stand a marshmallow's chance in hell of escaping without getting cooked some more. Despite my vow to go with you no matter where our path led us, huddling with you in the haunting shadows of that barren and unknown wilderness was more than my spirit could bear.

We went there together, but why exactly we could no longer tell.

In truth, a foundation for fire cannot endure without stone cold strength to support it. When we established our firepit in the hope of containing our flame, I brought pebbles and shattered boulders that anyone with experience knew were insufficient for the task at hand. I was an inadequate craftsman, carving a cavity of quarried walls that crumbled like long-lost ancient fortifications in a waving flagstone surrender. Little wonder that when you brought your torch to me there was skepticism in your eyes. You had seen failure before its time on enough previous occasions to know to insulate yourself against the inevitable blaze when my stonework failed to carry the weight.

V, when we predictably fell apart, there was no detonation, no spectacular fireworks to light up the night sky. Yet there was conflagration; after the blaze we stole moments to graft reality onto our dispositions like skin transplanted to heal the trauma of life-threatening burns. I expected third-degree heat from you but your furnace, neglected while your ardour cooled over time, had long ago run out of lumber.

V.

You could no longer stoke embers to initiate the combustion necessary to warm my shivering form.

Our campsite, however, was an inferno — though neither of us could blame the other for being the accelerant that reduced our sheltered lives to orphaned metal spikes imbedded in earth. The entwining bonds that supported the canvas upon which we painted our emotional projections were reduced to grimy soot. Nothing but ashes remained, and you were anxious to clear them out and start over once again. You secretly had your assurance in place all along and, once you (were) redeemed, it was time to rebuild.

When I took a hike at your behest for the final time, sullied soles grinding charcoal crystal blackness into newly broken trail, I remembered to scout the bushes for wild dangers before stepping too deeply into the brush.

A healthy respect for one's surroundings helps to avoid the deadliest of perils lurking just beyond the edge of awareness. §

T.

Terse: 1. free of superfluous words; concise in a polished, smooth way; succinct 2. brief or concise to the point of rudeness; curt

1.

Nothing lingers too long in your presence. You proceed at a precise clip. No wasted glares or confusion about your facial expressions. Emotions paint your face like they're college summer students. Colour coats situations like triple goose fed by the riverside. It's the way you (and they) were bre(a)d.

2.

You had no words to define what you felt. Vocabulary needed to catch up with experience. Working it out was a full-time job. No breaks from the feelings. No vacations from negative emotions. The boss was always screaming about someone not pulling their weight. No one to pick up the slack. Resentments advanced faster than skill sets. You struck. Out. At anyone.

You jabbed the bull blind.

You landed a heavy punch. Molars shattered in place of morals. Incisors split skins of cheeks, not fruits. Hit a psychic sore spot and roared at the sport of it. Labour caused the damage. Contusions and lacerations raw reminders of your violence.

To spar one needs a partner. I wasn't prepared to train you outside the ropes. Conundrum left both of us cornered: To exercise emotions meant going more rounds. Pound for pound, that battle proved tougher for you. It was impossible to successfully fight and advance through the division.

You tore away faster towards full detachment — left me hanging on to severed ropes.

3.

Every attempt at mutual engagement was tenuous. Occasionally grazing fingertips while setting up the pieces. Hungry for emotional sustenance. We ate up the lines of rank and file. The square perfect in its capacity to host. In this world, your moves first moved my heart white clean. My piece(s) the only blackness in my mind.

Over time you found, then refined, a strategy. Your mind progressed in three dimensions. The board remained complex beyond your comprehension. A talented yet circumscribed pawn. Every (k)night with the king courted conflict with the queen. Castle intrigue that played out by rook or by crook. The boss claimed superiority by any possible means. Left a mate vulnerable to being checked. An effective queen's gambit.

Poor pawn can never move back(ward) into safety.

It was never a game to me. I played along because I wanted you to win. I followed the rules for your sake. You were the object of the game. You were the definition of victory. Yours was the heart that had to experience the sensation of triumph. Keeping that at the forefront was the point. Scoring points was the only thing that mattered. But the boss chose to score cheap points at the forefront. Became addicted to the sensation of triumph by any means at hand. If it meant trampling your heart and breaking the rules, fine. Playing to win was the object of the game. My defeat was the definition of victory.

It was always a game to the boss.

4.

The king lacked protection. Taking him off the board was paramount. Spectators gathered round(s). Held their breaths. You threw your hands. Saw the sweat fly.

Concentration came whenever light flooded the square. Piece by piece, you had to stand and deliver. Cover your territory. Delight with your intelligence. Devastate with strategy divulged blow by blow. After each bruising battle, you were fit to be boxed.

The keys to the matter in unlocked ches(t)s. A litany of possibilities awaited each successive move. Grand masters always a(n upper)cut above. So, you countered and parried each aggressive incursion. Earned your elevated rankings. Knew that you measured up to the tale of the tape.

Mixed black and white figures in an orchestrated dance. Called the tune. Manipulated the outcome. Knew that, whether ring or board, you played to win.

Blood on the chessboard. Tears on a turnbuckle.

Pugilism with the boss's flair.

5.

Has your heart ever experienced a genuine sensation of triumph?

The truth is that the beauty in touching fingertips was offset by its infrequency.

The fight of your life was fixed from the start. Instead of the prize, you became the canvas. To triumph would have required stepping all over you. I chose to hang up my gloves and maybe fight another day. Under different circumstances. Ones where you were your own boss. So, I threw in the towel. Only one thought haunts my choices: Was shame or wisdom the victor when I forfeited?

Or did everyone lose? §

L.

Lamentation: the act of lamenting; outward expression of grief; esp., a weeping or wailing

From the first sharply inhaled breath drawn into your moist newborn lungs, we were half-baked flipsides on a cosmological hot plate. We were predestined to spit fire and burn down anything foolhardy enough to obstruct our paths. We erupted through crust and mantle and clay as dual seismic rocking of the spaces we inhabited. In our own separate settings and rhythms, we exhaled lava, and in our own spheres of influence our existences continue to reshape the world.

There was no way to envision the extent of interconnectedness in the earliest days of our epic epoch. Neither of us could possibly understand the correspondence of our revealed providences.

Our internal ferocity begat lakes of purifying fire that burst forth onto the earth's surface through fortuitous natural ruptures. A similarity in violent forces that repeatedly evacuated our smouldering cores reinforced the fraternity of our fractures. When refilled with incendiary ammunition, we knew how to breathe out with scorching, heated exhalations.

Had we happened to bubble to the earth's surface from the same Irish spring, our relations would teasingly have labelled us twins. The only features we shared with an isle of emerald were our shared descent from islanders and our greenness to the ways of the world. Nevertheless, being beings of radiance caused us to cast beams across scenes draped in black, green, and gold. The source of our ebullience at the site(s) of (our separate) terraforming tremors shone most brightly in our darkest moments. As expositional embodiments of post-enslaved chattel with the power to freely excoriate ecology beneath our footsteps, the melodies we composed were unequivocally unchained. We sang different songs but, like unrestrained thunder, they were always bangers that hit shit hard.

Throughout our journeys we've been shrouded one from the other by the curvature of surface distortions reminiscent of a globe. Truths were warped and directed away from us, concealed for nefarious reasons, done supposedly to protect us. These genealogical hustlers failed to grasp that it was others in the global sphere who would need protection from us. Daily disenchantments broiled our innards to liquid flame within the cauldrons that housed our devastations. When it was time to start dispensing wisdom, it emerged from grey matter that had been fried to a crisp by hot air blowing up our childhoods. The seared, hyper-pressurized contents of our cranial cavities divested their desires in divergent processes and still, despite every effort to the contrary, we independently evolved into similar species on opposite sides of continental divides.

As with all independent evolutions that emerge in distinct habitats, there were crucial variations in patterns that led to marginally different manifestations of genetically foregone conclusions. Shared fraternity fathered certain geothermal explosions at the base of our mountainous ambitions, yet our distinct localities stressed the significance of our sites of genesis. Our unique shaping due to the impacts of floating tectonic plates and nurturing meteorology proved beyond doubt that every aspect of one's origins combines with haphazard (un)predictability to generate a symphony of conceivable outcomes. Our instruments of transformation produced storms of elocutions as electric as Hendrix-smashed guitars and hooked every earlobe that picked up those insistent notes of creativity, punctuated by demanding charged silences, on the wind.

For it was in those pauses where the causes for applause became plausible. They meshed with the clap of trouble that clef(t) where you rested while pushing packs from the place where you lyrically blew people's wigs back. Putting in work that cleaved close to every line on the page revealed you as a street preacher when buoyed by the bounce of the bass. Your articulation was the ultimate equalizer, and you scorched a clear path for yourself, turning heavily on the gain. The reverberations of your quakes rendered the insufficiently reinforced to rubble. The congenitally unworthy cannot ever remain standing in the face of a natural phenomenon.

Though we are both beasts at peace with the inner rumblings we intermittently unleash upon an unsuspecting countryside, do you sometimes wonder what we could have done in closer proximity? If our lakes of fire found a foothold upon similar surface impressions, and creased the continent in an intricate interplay where we were the only ones to note the orchestration and conduct ourselves accordingly? If we had seized the wand and turned desert deciduous with exhalations of ash, and engraved furrows into shield rock to hollow hovels for rodents and carve kettles for the gatherings of birds?

Together we have the power to blot out the sun. I'm sure you've occasionally felt the urge — with the permanent extinction of peer peaks, fires dissipated, lava no longer to flow. I've heard you vent your rage, though I could not see you around the bend of our distorted sightlines. I have always felt every one of your violent entreaties to an environment not always conducive to your volcanic aspirations. Throughout time, I've sensed the subconscious echoing in language of rotation and orbit and tide and sundial shifting that acted as a constant reminder of your presence. I wonder if you have felt it too, though with you over there and me over here, we never discovered the patterns that would allow us to satisfactorily decode it.

Perhaps the day will come when we can have a moment of rap(port) to spit out burning truths, when the spoken word(s) of our semi-shared inheritance can shrink distances between us that predated the collisions that released molten magma from mantle. A moment may yet come when the commonality of our active states overwhelms the dissimilarity of our maternal emergence from steamy mists of creation.

It is in our births that we became connected, even if navel strings anchor us topologically to separate landscapes. And when we are extinct, the land will acknowledge us as part of the same fraternity, no matter how many more times we breathe fire, spill our ferocious innards to reshape our surroundings, and forever change the world.

Beyond the horizon, I can hear a distant rumble. I respond in kin(d). §

M.

Misunderstanding: 1. a failure to understand; mistake of meaning or intention 2. a quarrel or disagreement

Without you there is no commencement, no matriculation from pre to post, no graduating into the light, no passageway to the ranks of the intelligently conscious. The conveyance you provided me established my nascent footing in a world as ancient as Milky Way dust in a near-eternal cosmic echo. No Big Bang or bugle blasts announced me after my vocal chords took a few extra seconds to unstick from pre-emergent tracheal constriction. Muffled rifling to slo-mo Julian extrication to mewling to bellows — you wanted all the smoke. You got it with me. From that moment to now, you have watched me smoulder.

The alveoli inside my chest have always been combustible vessels carrying the messages of my upbringing; the ones in my mouth, cradles of transcendental creation. It is by your handiwork that I breathe, by God's that we aspire, rate of lingual pace torrid as a wind-stoked brushfire. Once it became clear they functioned as intended, no longer in bated-breath, semi-conscious suspension, the first embers dimly started to glow.

As a child, I devoured fibrous stalks that grew plentifully from garden variety containment — fields of fantasy and fiction that I danced through like a child of the corn. Before most others of my size and comportment could support the sport in each tome, long or short, you took time to decode symbols my stubby short fingertips traced with tentative yet determined purpose. At your knee, my consciousness learned first to toddle and then to walk under its own power. From there I booked it from preschool leisure to elementary exploration of my own burgeoning intellect, your hand steady on my shoulder as I figured out how to plant toes tipped with anticipation into the solid earth and begin to run (in the way of) my race.

At your knee, my consciousness learned first to cower and then to shrink from your power. In the long and the short of it, the threads of my existence were woven together under the pressure of your expert hands. Now, looking back, we can see how what was reaped was sewn. Beaten to a pulp, the drum rhythm, more resilient than the metallic timbre of horns, saved my skin more times than my memory cares to be tapped. Sore hips and wonky joints a chorus of disjointed locomotion, I no longer dance between the fibres but weave them myself — your handiwork written all over every one of my nouns, verbs, adjectives, and prepositions. Like a knee dull in the haystack of my remembrances, I genuflect at your influence over me while hoping the backward flight ends with a cushioned landing. I do not wish to revisit any of the pain. Old garden-variety fibres dried out but I must trust they still provide refuge.

Innumerable challenges materialize progressively upon thresholds that straddle what was and what continues to become. You gave me a start, with energy that still leaps within me, propelling emotion and voice and instinct. With the benefit of your own hindsight, my movements were destined to cross purposes with decisive intention. You are marionette thread bearer — it dances bidden by strings without form, vanishingly effective and forever enduring. Pathways present themselves by leaps and bounds to taunt and tantalize — endless options, selected like reggae tracks at a sweaty Caribbean fete, wheeling yet fated never to come again. Melodies echo and fade once a doorway is chosen, broadest vision of time Atreides narrowed, fight against stagnation in favour of the boldest possible course of action. Poignant discovery.

Clearly, you have always stood guard, transitional figure, headed both towards the future with eyes firm on past impacts. On this middle ground, you remain, Janus-like, guide for heartstrings still tugged by occasional loving interventions that mark profound passages. What do your eyes digest from your perch as they freely scan the flowing estuaries of your history? Which yearnings burned so brightly as they strung together your marionette vignettes that the screen of your internal consciousness was forced to exhale them before you suffocated from the smoke? What of the reeds that define your soul?

The Moses you (th)rushed from the banks of your memories was the culmination of your decades of investment, richness personified, symbol of your emotional wealth. Through your double consciousness, the blur of society's rebuttal made you cross on deeper examination. You kept making a stand as a witness to the badgering that was brought to bear, ignorant of truth, affront to justice, runaway entrapment of a blackness bleak in its accurate veracity. Enslaved to the realities of then and now, destined to desert one place to find promise in another, you created the transcendence realized in the pull of your preoccupations. Preordained supreme opposition symbolized in auspicious beginnings. Only once the limitless vocabulary within your liminal boundaries were you able to exhale — to embrace the ignition. Through you, alight, my passions burn. And flow.

M.

You have never fully comprehended any of this, how I have come to be pillar, radiant guide. It is not that I have done this but rather that you are its embodiment — in the reflection of your inflections, the amplification of your ardour, the frenetic fulfillment of your frequencies, the verbalization of your subconscious expressions. You have procreated what is both evident and imperceptible, transient and permanent, while permitting the penetration of your power into the ever-expanding universe of our mutual possibilities. One does not grasp themselves with their own palms when reaching for what makes sense in this world.

Instead, bear both what has come and what is with courage, while sparking each consecutive moment of unfolding actualization. Guard the doors, begin at the beginning, keep movement in static reverberation, and remember to breathe on the remnants of what is about to be. With you, every heartbeat is a brand-new January with the weight of your symbols sunken into earth, planted firmly, as aspirations of fire animate your heavenly glow.

Never to be doused or snuffed out. §

P.

Perdition **1. ARCHAIC complete and irreparable loss; ruin** 2. THEOL. a) the loss of the soul; damnation b) hell

1.

Hellacious P: Where your hands work themselves into a frenzy, the world bleeds.

Traversing this random path's three most recent stepping stones caused us to reach you by skipping two symbols — the scream of NO in grating friction of flung-open gates upon our arrival punctured the silence. Destruction awaited on the other side where persistence hinged on a vivified reset after disruptive palpitations. Arriving at your side before completed preparation was to choke on the venom of un-slaughtered serpent, newfangled danger at the point of violence. As its discharge pumped, one prayed to avoid capillary capitulation. Only one vessel can carry you (to the) hereafter.

Some cycles should never become venal carriages for your marauding emotional destruction. Cowardice is a coin you spend well even when lacking sufficient internal leverage to compound self-interest. Cut and run, if you must, to save (your) face (value) no matter how much collateral (damage) is required — there's a conviction you've always been able to take to the bank. Bruising impacts of your feckless selfishness that stretch beyond your reach are criminally withdrawn from your everyday realities. There can be no retrieval of the bounty you swiped, of what others have treasured deeply. In material ways, the reverberations of your breathlessly obtuse wretchedness are immaterial to our recovery. We remain eternally in the red no matter the fashion in which your resentments circulate. Your ambitions latch thirstily to other's lifeblood before swallowing their wholesomeness whole.

The oxygen-starved must rage ferociously at your heedless ignorance.

Why, like Barabbas, do you receive reprieve from the consequences of your barbarity — ancient grievances passed over with a crowdsourced pardon in favour of murdering what we see as sanctified? What goes around surely must come back around again. The rest of us, denied the sweet sustaining produce of the body by your malignancy, await with growing interest the moment your *mort* gauge finally comes full circle.

• • •

Perdition 1. ARCHAIC complete and irreparable loss; ruin **2. THEOL. a) the loss of the soul; damnation** b) hell

2.

Nightmarish P: They say the devil is a liar. You must be, at greatest distance, a first cousin — never removed.

My mouth sours with distaste at the thought of having once savoured your severities and thought them to be sweet fruit of the vine. It is said that human tastebuds can alter over time. One year's delectable culinary delight can dramatically transmogrify into the next year's deadly anaphylactic shock. Eternal allergy to your scent, flavour, and accents renders me unable to find any redeeming quality to be extracted from beneath your pestilent skin. Such contaminated fruit cannot ever be worth the squeeze.

To satisfy the desire to experience tastiness blessed into the body of every believer requires genuflection at the altar of godliness. You, faithless, sought to steal what was not rightfully yours. Sadly, you were granted access out of depressive weakness despite the prevailing knowledge that the fit was not right for purpose. Mismatch of key and keyhole was predestined to result in mangled metal and pounded pine. A failure of openness. No way to pass from there to here.

Even in my process of attempting to backstop my way to a shutout, you manipulated your way into a score.

Your stickhandling was much more skilled than previous, your control of your personal athleticism at the tip top of your form. You descended upon me with determination to find space that had been denied to you until that moment, unyielding, disinterested in anything that resembled making a pass. Despite strong opposition, you insinuated your way between my goalposts, determined to slap the puck into the goal. Your successful breakdown of the defence led to a penalty shot that you savoured with aplomb. Your celebration was an abomination to my instincts, a defiling of my resistance, in defiance of all propriety. You had no business using me for sport, having turned my surface to smooth chill iciness. And yet, there you were, smirking at my traumatic defeat.

The scenario loops through my being at the most unfortunate and unwanted of moments. Like flipping through stations on a cable box, there is it, flashing across my screen. Replay of the miscues of the week, of the season, of the decade … stretch the timeline and it snaps me painfully, unexpected sting more agonizing than rebounding childhood rubber bands. Your blade gouged me with your razor turn, indentation indelible, no Zamboni remedy in sight, the spray and shards of your sharp shower of self-loathing, disgust, and shame a shock to the system every time on recollection as it was in the moment. No matter how often I attempt to change the channel, your self-satisfied condemnation of my own needs keeps on blazing LCD bright on the screen behind my eyes.

• • •

Perdition 1. ARCHAIC complete and irreparable loss; ruin 2. THEOL. a) the loss of the soul; damnation **b) hell**

3.

Torturous P: The steady drip of memory on the forehead of my immobilizing emotional imprisonment is your everlasting legacy on the pathway to Hades.

Like all fiendish fraudsters, you're adept at deflecting your own culpability while simultaneously seducing others with deceptively charismatic vivacity. You find energy for life in the false hope of death, mistruth personified and cloaked in Jezebel allure.

The construct within which you exist from day to day is a vacuous sinkhole for virtue, word salad on the smorgasbord buffets your mendacity renders unnourishing, disintegrated stairway to heaven — pillars of salt that melt away at the slightest warmth or outpouring of emotion. An escort for manipulated souls who seek solace in the poison of your tongue, the echo of my NO should ring in your deafened ears. Instead, it registers nowhere within the realm of the righteous. Disconnect between saved and damned, compound and bloody, fracture of my wholeness a relic of your past indignities and artifices, allergic to healing and insanely painful.

May the flames of your hatreds consume the pyres of your flesh, your untruths comatose when committed to paper, your cunning sham of a conscience your eternal undoing. May you be left with nothing but ash in your mouth. Try to speak then.

Let your breath do nothing except feed the earth-cleansing inferno. Reduce you to nothingness. You dishonour the dust. §

B.

Belligerent: 1. at war; designating or of a state recognized under international law as being engaged in a war 2. of war; of fighting 3. seeking war; warlike 4. showing a readiness to fight or quarrel: a belligerent gesture or tone

On the heels of hideous P, it would have been nice to write about your charming and endearing features, the right elegance of the curves at your side, the firmness left in your spinal disposition, the power of your secondary position in the alphabet. I ache to appeal to the gentler angels in my conscience, exhorting exultations on your loveliness, detailing your beauty in breathless verbal gushing. Would it not be lovely to speak with thrill rather than ill?

Instead, the mere comprehension of you sets my plasma to a roiling boil, desperate to smash platelets over your cellular fragment of a heart. The bloodletting would be ugly to regard.

It's amazing how smoking hot you think you are, even in the face of overwhelming evidence to the contrary. You — lit on fire, bile bilious, insides at imminent and constant risk of a slow burn — exist blithely unaware of your inability to be a credible source of heat.

Where you contact the natural world, you feed on the environment's oxygen to pollute it, singed by ignited flaky dryness and marred by a sticky tar personality. At the opposite point where you draw (from) breath, no filter can protect flesh from the fetid foulness that corrupts to your core. Every exhalation delivers another abominable representation of what it means in this world to not give a shit. Each inhale allows more fuel for infernal internal dialogue to persist unabated. The full act permits your unhealthy growth, cancerous, to infiltrate the atmosphere with rhythmic persistence. There is nothing benign about such malignantly vocal bellicosity.

Your verbs are born to fight, adjective to slay any noun adversary, every utterance a death sentence that solely speaks the vocabulary of the pettily vindictive.

Unable to claim Q's motive of revenge against oppression to build an indestructible legacy, you quarrel without constructive purpose. The entwining bonds that supported the canvas upon which V painted emotional projections, eventually reduced to grimy soot, never existed between us, B. You are an entirely different sort of aggressor, a negative magnification of the vindictive at its combative extreme, the ash created by your profanities the product of an inequitable and incalculable value quotient. You devise new diabolical ways to divide, so the sum of your severities can multiply wounds inflicted, exponentially.

There may have been aspirations that you g(r)asped for yearningly along the branches of bronchial trees, but such exertions always left you breathless. Now that your humanity has turned to ash, you no longer hold the capacity to breathe in rarified air. You became the dustbin of history no one wishes to explore, allergic to your remembrance, immune to contemplation of your existence.

Where you've gone, deliberate forgetfulness follows out of sheer self-preservation.

Since your words hold nothing for me, the least I can do in return is hold back my salubrious rebutting soliloquies and devote as few words to addressing you as possible. Repulsing the repellant is especially exhausting when one can refuse to choke down your internal make-up under pressure. Your ashen aims do nothing except leave a putrid taste in my mouth as I fight the full-throated reflex to gag and expectorate the unexpected.

If you remain capable of feeling a (community's) pulse, I know you know you're already beat.

You unfailingly, successfully choose violence at every opportunity for human interaction: at work, while resting, during play, upon sunrise, at sunset, out loud, in silence, in the depths of winter, amidst the heights of summer, midspring, as we fall — never for good, always for ill. Ravenously, you feed on vitriol as if it were nectar, sweet and succulent, dripping and dribbling from the corners of your mouth as you speedily slurp with no consideration that you might move more slowly and take your time.

Battling the urge to engage with you has grown simpler over time. Once convicted with your pointlessness, it's easy not to get smoked out. Your attack bombs and turns you back to dust — a dead end for a deadheaded pugilist, destined in a final jab to spar with shadows. §

N.

Naughty: 1. OBS. wicked; bad; evil 2. not behaving properly; mischievous or disobedient: used esp. of children or their behavior 3. showing lack of decorum; improper, indelicate, or obscene

You are creation in carnal form.

Innate expression of my deepest desires dominates your impulses as surely as your magnetic attractiveness imprisons my urges and locks them permanently in your erotic embrace, without hope of release, parole, or pardon. Once inserted, the key may only unlock the doors to your soul's unspoken demands upon me and nothing more.

This cell bars nothing.

The only break to which we are ritually subjected is inevitable denouement following the climax, successive stories that beg to be told aloud, persistent, insistent, vocally demonstrative in the plot of our rising action and restful in the gentility of re-energizing epilogue. The way you turn my pages while you crack my spine provides endless stimulation between hardcovers. Each word you whisper into my shivering form are divinations to elevate my vitality. Every special phrase and reminiscence must be dog-eared for anticipatory reconnection, never forgotten, that encourages doggedly determined re-consumption.

Where you've left your mark, I lie pressed to breathlessness between lingually lascivious sheets, readying to recommence. Flip to double page spreads smouldering passions wide. The tome of your tongue burns bright: You are what happens when smoke signals convert to a show. A whirling dervish of spiritual resonance flutters from the pages, swirls dust to enveloping clouds of allure. You cloak yourself in loin-entrancing mystery as the audience gasps in repressive desperation. You can be felt, experienced, observed, imitated, worshipped, yet never truly understood. My body yearns for sustenance from your flesh.

To sate you is to be slated for subsistence on sensations that can never be exclusively mine. You seduce the molecules suspended invisibly silent everywhere my body moves, so why would any other set of eyes fail to widen under your engendering gaze? Those not invited to taste the air rarified by your pheromones may as well male it in at the starting line. A bridged version of my struggle against your chemically charged charms leads inevitably like luring breadcrumbs along the path of least resistance: to the ties that bind, the motion of the ocean, the commotion, the languid float of the ship on waters calm in the aftermath of your somatic hurricane.

Lustily, I return to you, addictive cyclone, in search of your eye yet knowing the ferocity of the blowing winds and saturation from the storm surge are what intrigue me and swing me repeatedly around your turbulent centre. You are full destruction of my inhibitions and invitation into your chaos. Turned into storm chaser measuring the depth of the heat you suck from the ocean; no watch or warning can keep me from plumbing your depths to get a full sense of the magnitude of your power.

Tempestuously, you twist, sultry and stormy, your comportment conceding nothing. No matter which way I spin, your pretty roulette pattern board has already held any possibilities I present and rendered every single bet I lay as misplaced amusement. I propose to you as a final attempt at saving grace, double or nothing, and your arching eyebrow betrays a play that you know must surely pay off. The house (that can somehow accommodate us) wins.

A new chapter begins. The sea's heat increases with a velocity that can incubate a typhoon. Your passion lays down a sentence that I am utterly powerless to appeal. Key jangles in hole. Captured.

Take me to where your escorting hand spreads the expanses of your insides and enthralls with the narratives of your steps. Suspend disbelief at the suppleness of your skin for several breaths. The depth of you draws the attention away from the full map of your journey and for my incarceration within your passions I must be expert cartographer.

Allow me to trace your lines with my fingertips — let them mingle with your meridians to learn curves unassociated with the extremities of hip explorations we've previously been armed with. Teach me the coded meaning of symbols in your legend, the demarcation of elevations and valleys of your continental breadth, the unexplored and underexplored contours of your topography. If you can be experienced as a volume, allow it to be an atlas that acts as a guide to decipher your most significant manifestations. Or, even better, permit me to caress the corners of your glossy geographic dimensions to analyze and create my own interpretations.

In your most honest and vulnerable formation, you are an open book. And through the solidification of understanding in the process of acquiring key knowledge, the facility at the heart of your embrace ignites the stories we scribe in blood and ink and pencil and bytes into the permanence of our conjoined universes.

Your passions kiss me with rapturous flame and the shape of my inner world is forever transmuted. We become animated scripts with the playfulness of Shakespeare and the lilt of Rumi, the concreteness of Descartes, and the observant perspective of Gladwell. And yet, we can never give up on the hours and hours of carnal combination of bass and alto, exhorting the skies to harmonize, the cycle of surge and calm and climax and re-energizing perpetually unbroken. The combination of depth of emotional exploration and libidinous comprehension is the tipping point that replaces saving grace with doubled loops in an eternal cyclonic reverie.

N.

Your skin is a treasure map that only I can read, your flesh a prison I wish never to break free from, your lips the conveyance of a heat that powers my soul on titanic journeys. When we place our heads together and share a language that only we can g(r)asp, the air charged and spiced with a brew only you and I can concoct, push me down and shackle me to your body with an impenetrable grip.

And set me to whirl again. §

A.

Anger: 1. a feeling of displeasure resulting from injury, mistreatment, opposition, etc., and usually showing itself in a desire to fight back at the supposed cause of this feeling 2. OBS. pain or trouble

1.

Like a popular podcast, where should we begin?

Recall our genesis, where the world first presented itself with antiseptic brightness in a sterile environment and then failed to turn off the spotlight. For decades. Excessive luminosity burns. Learning to live incandescently can leave one permanently on the spot. Light in the pocket. Book a bankrupting one-way trip while wrapped in dermal organ overbaked to a crisp — the epitome of pain. Full of hypocrisy and deception, betrayal and mendacity, a frustration that marks like a mangled tattoo and is just as aggravating to look at day after day after day.

We carry the burdens of initial resentments baked into the eight digits daubed onto a tiny slip of blue government-issued paper. It was almost as if the commencement of our existence was a smear that defiled the very face of civilization.

Black globs and speckles flung against the white picket fence leave those standing guard patterned with Dalmatian ambiguity. To be seen in such a state is internally conflicting: To live as a fence is to plant yourself firmly in place and fail to move forth; to live as the paint reflects creativity in full flight. Movement and inertia; forward progress violently interrupted by the rigidly immovable. To accept both as equally valid requires challenging the post('s) position while encouraging the paint to make the best of where it finds itself.

For half a millennium, the detritus from these front yard collisions built up within the paint bucket in unseen spirals that were passed from parent to child, like Jamaican relay teams passing the baton. While we claim victory (with)in the race(s), others berate us for proudly crossing the line. We've managed to perfect the Pyrrhic with disturbing efficiency — running away from shotgun blasts, working together to come out ahead, claiming the laurels with an entertainer's flair, only to have Olympic-sized successes disparaged and denigrated. We are the black licorice of Candyland, flavour-filled nightmares, our raciness expectorated like chewed-up tobacco juice, not to everyone's taste. Even in the areas where we dominate, the time is nigh for reversal.

Ah well. It's been a good run.

Listen up, A: Since the very beginning, we've been flipping tables, screaming at the moon with unbridled ferocity, boiling rouge-tinted fluids behind eyelids projecting pain beyond our lashes. We are (sub)conscious brutality given form, feeling, and fight. To live in such a state with constancy and intensity requires a commitment most humans lack the gumption to summon through their fragility, self-absorption, and fear. We live a Gatlin existence, which can lead us deep into places where our projectile discontentment should never be cranked at pace.

Born six years apart on June 6, we were fed a devilishly repetitive diet: "Here comes trouble," "Get outta my way!" and "I'll give you something to cry about...." Our pentagonal ruthlessness was born ready for hand-to-hand combat. We subsist on the vicious, hydrate on the terror of the cowering prostrate, prone to bouts (of rage) where the boxed are encircled and their bells roundly rung without mercy.

But do not mistake our diabolical obsession with punishing retribution as innate. It was bred into us as a natural response to this world, roasting us in our skins, broiling our passions from the inside out. Every half-baked scheme, charcoal-dusted decision, and acrid word hurled in disgust and frustration was a bitter pill swallowed and regurgitated for public examination. The vomitous treatment of our innards resulted in a bilious disregard for those beyond our reckoning. We cannot hold down while being held down. The ferocious need to break free from our inept and cruel antagonists occupies the full scope of our ocular inhalations. We must see to it that we are not the targets of the spit.

Time to cook up a new course while ensuring we are not amongst those destined to get served.

Anxiety: 1. a state of being uneasy, apprehensive, or worried about what may happen; concern about a possible future event 2. PSYCHIATRY an abnormal state like this, characterized by a feeling of being powerless and unable to cope with threatening events, typically imaginary, and by physical tension, as shown by sweating, trembling, etc. 3. an eager but often uneasy desire: anxiety to do well

2.

We apprehend new truths every time we scour broken memories like slippery chinaware downed on solid tile — there is beauty in our shattered bits, and the promise of tedious future reassembly work to reconstitute a whole. Perceived inability to persevere is a clueless ghoul in self-loathing clothing. Exhibit the mustard to affect the affirmation of your agency because we're plum out of time for excuses. The toil and trouble in every overheated spell of our staged engagement risks scalding anyone who gets too close. We've been burnt so many times. Since it is said that hurt people hurt people, we must act to avoid that bill of damages evidenced in the hurlyburly of our history of violence.

All this unceasing adrenaline activation comes at a cost, A. Living with a hair trigger wicked fever burbling in our subconscious leaves us Fosbury jumpy, ready to flop into the closest soft pit to burrow to its bottom as rodent Gonzales quickly as possible. We're talking about a wrap sheet long enough for a king, in which we've made our own bed. Seek out the dormant view like Brother John and endeavour to put our disease to sleep. Dive headlong into the waters of the (un) well. Fail to make a splash. Just bucket.

Like dispelling recollection of a fearful apparition in the blackest abysses of rapid eye movement, it's easier dreamt than done.

A fraught discomfiture pitches us into unbridled panic when we reflect on all the ways we've been forced to hang onto the rope. Push the rope. Knot the rope. Hang from the rope. Rope-a-dope. Slip the rope. Develop the skills to do all these things or that's all she wrote.

Without an apple as sinful as Adam's, we could never speak well enough to breathe in the hope of our own future Eden. Each taste awakens ever more of our awareness of our mortality. Once roused from ignorance, the seed in our open eyes at the core of the matter can never again be denied. Tension snakes through our reasoning, leaves us helpless in the face of the fear. We cannot smite the eyes of our enemies if we lack the fortifications from which to raise our arms. Embracing self-reliance cannot be a temporary fling.

When we resurface from our hiding place and turn to face the blinding light that we have never learnt to avoid, our retinas overwhelmed by the flood they cannot completely decipher, the only option is to close our eyes and say a prayer. Ask for security and comfort. Guidance and strength. Plead for understanding and grace. Appeal for wisdom and composure. Seek all these things and more to overcome every anxiety and provocation, every threat and injury, whether imagined or real. Implore every scrap of support in our exhortation to the powerful trinity: me, myself, and I.

We are ready. §

S.

Sanctimony: 1. affected piety or righteousness; religious hypocrisy 2. OBS. sanctity

We used to be tight once.

Back then, as far as I was aware, hypocrisy was a stranger to you. I was not. We styled spaces to bend minds that generated critical applause for creative citations meant to gin up generations and support wide exposure of nascent literary sensations (mostly Canadian, not *français* Caribbean or from farther afield). Masters of the times within word's play and arbiters of moments to mete out sanctions for tardy terminations, we capitalized on curated verbal collisions, by the by, in ways monumental enough to raise mercury. At times it felt like the caloric venting of heated exhalations could power the sunrise. It was as if the resourceful energies these cultivated excavations unearthed could be mined endlessly.

As partners we were married to the game as truly as you were bound within the lingual twigging of your own nest, feathered with letters and loose leaves for the comforts of mutual habitude. An unacknowledged part of me was low-key envious of your context. Looked like a wonderful world from which to take wing. Fly in the ointment was coming but at this point, there was nothing but *plein-air* where we could branch out — paint our ambitions across the limitless expanses of our own industriousness and verve. Our interactivity and joint purpose held promise redolent with the prospect of future success. I took it on, came to the nest to revitalize with you, felt the warmth of your friendship feed my creative soul.

In tandem, we interwove patches of fabric that tied together to support a multitude's weight with their resilient threads. Our ministrations netted a bounty that could feed more than those nourished as recounted in fourteen verses in the book of John. Despite your categorical denial of the existence of divine intervention, for years it was like we caught far more than two lonely fish, broke well in excess of five loaves of bread, and drank like we were four chapters deep into the well-watered wine of Cana. The facts of our collaborative triumphs are gospel truth spread by crafty disciplines across the entire land. So many were well-fed by it that they could not help but know its provenance.

As providence would have it, you were used by a higher power to cast Thomasian doubt upon my share of the wealth we excavated together. Irony deficiency is not your issue. Any anemic responses to that which afflicted the blood of the corps(e) passed you by without slowing down at the rubberneck. Cut off from circulatory flow, tight as a tourniquet, I was cursed to a fate of deliberate atrophy through malicious negligence. Your malevolent grip yanked the ends of life tighter around me and your vanity palpated my sensitive private spaces to prep them for stabbing. The object was to administer general anesthetic, then bleed me out with a contaminated blade jammed into paralyzed flesh while the whole lay unconscious, oblivious to treachery inflicted under cover of darkness.

The tell-tale wound hemorrhaged and turned gangrenous, as you intended. Yes, it did. But then I did a thing that was insufferably annoying to you: Though my health was out on a limb, I stubbornly refused to shrivel up and die at your hand.

You sought to make me lamb on the altar of your (self-) righteousness and sacrifice me to your vile false stand-in idols that pass for your worshipped deities. Your lack of belief in a supreme being failed to deter you from behaving like disreputable Pharisees in the temple. Woe unto you, scribes — like a sacrifice made on a modern Drake stage my underground expressions set the bar high. You disrespect the temple with your creative blasphemies when you condemn others for sin yet self-select a path of wickedness. You can never be justified if the temple is only meant to serve as venue to unpardonable pronouncements where you cast unverified and indecent aspersions with imperturbable assurance.

For it is said: "Do not judge, or you too will be judged. For in the same way you judge others, you will be judged, and with the measure you use, it will be measured to you."

Self-satisfied, you continued to eat at the expense of people exploited by the new selfishness motivating your ventures into the mines. Like a glutton filled to bursting with sloth, you were too lazy to clean the inside of the bowl you filled to overflowing and the cup you used to keep you drunk on your own supply yet were fastidious enough to keep a cloth handy to polish their outsides to a sheen. One must maintain appearances. You clutch the rag with pious affect, pleading to all within earshot of your entitlement to gorge, while the spaces you once fed calories to power the sunrise starved for something other than your hot air. In seeking to become the sun, you set your own path to failure.

Slowly, as the full body came back to reality, you realized the effort to excise a troublesome extremity led to mortal jeopardy for the whole corps(e). The ointment contaminated by the insects you crushed lost its ability to heal. Your bowl's inner filth is no place to prepare life-saving treatment; your cup a pestilent vessel from which to pour a salving tonic. The poison spread farther and farther with each pump of the heart(less), delivering death to each organ, all the muscles, every gland and duct and ligament, the full constellation of bones. You scrambled to find a cure, but realized too late that if once-healthy organs start to shut down, there is no escape from the inevitable. The cascading consequences of your misdiagnosis and maltreatment, executed with egotistical self-assuredness and pompous exhibitionism at the start of this heinous procedure, cannot now be undone. You were never a legitimate surgeon. Quackery kills.

A plague came home to you, shattering your context, and I was low-key filled with relieved *schadenfreude*. When your wings dipped, you couldn't avoid losing control of your balance and crashing to earth. I was grateful to no longer be attached to you when the sun taught you a vital Icarus lesson. Wax nostalgic all you want; the sunrise wants no part of your monument to raised mercury turned terrestrial toxin. Like a canary, you should have known what happens if you cease mining gold and dig for coal instead. The game wants a divorce.

No — it wants an annulment.

We used to be tight once, but now we are as loose as leaves that float forlornly to earth from the branch that struggles to hold your barely intact discomfort of mutual habitude. The message in this parable is that un-curated verbal collisions lead to tardy termination at the site of perceived capitalizations. Your ending was predictable, the shredding of the net a certainty, your moral bankruptcy preordained. For your sake, I wish it were possible to pray for your soul's salvation, but frankly, that's just too much for the godless to expect.

As the righteous once said: With the measure you use, it will be measured to you. And it has found you to be about one hundred and eighty units short. §

F.

Forgiveness: 1. a forgiving or being forgiven; pardon 2. inclination to forgive or pardon

I intuited early that epic (high)tales of your paintbrush-stroked shortcomings would need to be told. Thanks to you, I was born a storyteller yanked by a discordant leash into life with post-mature conscious contemplation carved into my newborn animation. You played your (de)part(ure) well. They say that history is written by the victor. Hue goes to the heart of the issue; compassion, beaten, gets brained. Throw a (cala)bash to celebrate and watch me bleed.

Pen strokes to capture your impact feel reminiscent of lashings from long ago abuses the world cynically shrouds in shade. Full solar eclipse includes absences from nascent *naissance* with knock-on effects that echo with plaintive cries that shatter illusions of bliss. For nearly two score years, I scoured the past for glimpses of your support, found only pigs scouring the soil to bake in the excretable in your footsteps in the sand. It was not your goal. I got the point(s) anyway.

Dear shadow, there can be no turning back.

Only four words preface these disconsolate keystrokes: Where have you been? In your absence, my fingers have transmuted a million thoughts into complex conversations. A quadrillion letters with more character than you've injected into my plot stain (im)pressed *feuilles* that sing(le) out the arias of my soul. Life turned soap opera, coronated my young, bold, and beautiful restlessness with a dynasty of east ender angst, where scars burrow deep to deposit enduring plaques of resentment in my atria. Such reminiscences remain in heavy circulation as I vainly search for a trunk line to your exculpation. I understand that doing nothing is hazardous to my health.

At its root, I want most to heal.

The weight of numerous iniquities carries loads in your psyche — crippling pounds that must leave your cortex incapable of proceeding proudly apace. As age takes its toll, the price gets higher with each passing signpost. Do you tire with each new shock? It must take more and more energy to absorb each incidental blow; the creaks, sputters, and stutters an urgently flashing indicator of your need to repair the multitudinous damages your cerebrum inflicts upon itself and its environment. To lighten your load would be to equip yourself with the fuel to make it to the end of the line, would it not? Time for a checkup. From the neck up.

This line of thinking collars me as I contemplate the likelihood that your Waze guide headlong towards a similar fate to yours. When brains attack, heredity twists and turns along a path already plotted by the algorithm. Best not to believe that you chart a different route when your starting point blatantly betrays a predetermined destination not entirely of one's own choosing. Take health(y) care not to get carted away.

To get the best results, the alignment of my angle of attack with an optimal outcome must overcome your iffy lies. I'm experienced enough now to understand the rules, to comprehend the game's pitfalls and hazards, to swing with a little extra loft to get me on my fair way. Your past shows me that you occasionally consign me to unplayable uphill situations that bogey bruise my ability to gain ground. The eagle-eyed can spot what's not completely up to par, so it demands courage to take my scorecard into the clubhouse. In the end, what's the point in playing if there's no way for me to avoid the curse of a high handicap? Is this how your penalty strokes dictate how my round ends before I even begin?

Despite respect for recent developments in your short game, I cannot depend on a mulligan when it comes to you. I must dodge your ego strokes if they are putting me in danger.

This has been the problem all along — it coloured us both at inception and still influences our self-perceptions. I see now that you gave me everything you've got. I resent it.

It flew forth from me to contaminate the pool into which I dove without option in pursuit of a lane to victory. Winning wasn't my destiny; I wish it wasn't the future I begat that had to take the loss. Their chances got all wet in the deep end in ways that didn't suit. I stare googly-orbed and ashamed, uncomfortably aware of the washout I foresee with eyes irritated and burning.

Still, yours is the paintbrush that originally dabbled in the palette that divined the course of my lifeblood, so it is to you I must go to find absolution. Pain bleeds from gaps in my memory that you should yet do not inhabit, spectacular sights unseen that gnaw at crevices in my self-concept. To salve those wounds is to solve the mysteries that led to the bite marks I inflicted upon myself. There is no justice, just us and the past and the present that this moment provides that was almost taken away in a single stroke.

If my being is a gift, yours are the hands that gave it to me. To release ego in exchange for peace is the only stroke (of genius) I ever wish to experience in the shadow of our prior absences.

You can keep the rest, especially if it helps me preserve my mental health. §

C.

Compassion: sorrow for the sufferings or trouble of another or others, accompanied by an urge to help; deep sympathy; pity

When we first met, the season was late summer, the reason had yet to be revealed, and our lifetimes were waiting patiently to be more fully lived.

I, accustomed to environs filled with pontification, welcomed the knowledge you carried with the altruistic motivation of helping a peer. Once elementally introduced, we could not have conjured a combination more fascinating in the laboratory of the maddest of scientists. The chemical combination that spurred instant smiles and instinctive mutual understanding was as basic as they come. Synthesis of personal compatibilities was near instantaneous. Our reactions have never ceased to ignite imaginations or drive creative juices in constant flow.

Even as the substance of our compound communion spawned previously unknown possibilities, methodological discipline did not permit it to cross over into the physical realm. You've broken bread with me countless times without breaking down the boundaries that might lead to regretful rites of reconciliation. I confess that there were moments where exploratory curiosity nearly overtook me, but you never wavered from the path our collective energies initially chose — no penance required. Your intentions married well with your actions, so it was easy for me to confirm fealty and devotion. With friendly feelings of thanksgiving, as if called to reinforce each other's reciprocal faith under holy orders, we pronounced last rites on any potential mutual baptisms of blessed bodies by elevated blood.

Christ, that was such a long time ago.

Before ambition raised you up on eagle's wings, the direction of your pilgrimages took you west into a wild unknown. Walls that formed effective barriers to the sea could not halt your advance as you burrowed to an inlet that robbed the sun of sightlines to see you sweat. Your path illustrated the extent of the innate genius revealed to you like a mysterious ring in a shire. An embarrassing wealth of riches have poured forth from your nimble mind — enough to fill aquaria for those consigned to fishing for the truth in others' waters. As always, you were keen to be the guide cutting through the doldrums of ignorant unknowing. You just kept swimming until you found your Nemo on a mysterious island with an exterior glistening and slick, wetsuit skin-tight against your elements.

Diving deep into his ocean, you snorkelled at scuba depth, choking each infatuated molecule into flooded lungs.

He proved as fictional as your ability to breathe twenty thousand leagues under the sea. You drowned just a little bit with every inhalation. It took a very long time for you to realize that you, siren song–seduced, were miscast as a mermaid.

In the interim on a rim of fire, the water at your disposal at low ebb kept the smokescreen at a manageable level. Proceeding as if there was no warning in the sulphur emitted from the exhaust at your rear, you barnstormed like it would never overwhelm you. So long as the shield in front of you remained clear, stay the course. The walls of this seen barrier look like they could be broken down with a swift *jiu-jitsu* kick, as diminutive an impediment as your *rösti*-wrapped *adobo*-seasoned stature may appear to the uninitiated. Daringly undaunted, with an inner glow fiery bright yet cool to the touch, you charged forward into the unknown with an ache of nervous anticipation in your heaving chest.

An incredible series of gifts came to you from the father — a son that filled you like the Holy Spirit at a Pentecostal jubilee. Your first fruit was an admirable guardian angel, a shining spiritual headlamp that cut through the darkness of your world, who caused your heart to arch and soar in divine uplifting. The second blessing was an adorned and most holy corona, an embodied bacchanal of intellectual brilliance, bedazzling like a night sky borealis. The completion of the trinity came in the form of a warrior-guide able through feminine wiles to steer you beyond bullish humours and out of his entangling intrigues that constrain your freedoms.

By the time you begrudgingly accepted that he was only half a man, you'd already followed the thread of glittering jewels laid out to lead you from the entrapping labyrinth. After a minute or two, your thesis came to you. To slaughter the beast is to recognize what behooves us to acknowledge once adversity has been put to rest — walking in lockstep with the light sometimes requires one to take the bull by the horns. Under the protection of saviours, a soul was salvaged for the glory of goodness, all while never losing the empathy behind your forward-looking gaze. No bull.

In effecting your emotional emancipation, you soared above the fray — fully authentic, darling, and beloved.

• • •

Now I watch you, tongue knotted, as your unfettered freedom leads you to capture a new heart, happily entangled in fanned feathers unfurled after the heat of fiery rebirth. Tuck, roll, dip, and dive in open air to feel the rush in an intricate dawn-hour illumination. Sense the gently warming sun and feel the parallels line up within your own flesh. When the beauty of your internal synthesis was given a new lease, you chose to fully occupy it. With claws bared and in delicate balance, you soar in full command of your range, in protective mode over your progeny, ready for anything. To have once feared the bull's horns makes you ever sensitive to where and when you choose to dig in with strength. Clawing back is discarded therapy for the unhealed. You, as always, are razor sharp.

Ambition translates to wisdom in a thousand scenarios, and you are a living Rosetta stone. Thanks to you, the hieroglyphs of my own emotional confusion seem solvable — Watson daftness given a swift Sherlock comeuppance. Self-preservation is an ultimate act of love, and my pulse suspends with the hope of maintaining this disposition indefinitely. Proceed with amber. Though there is an appeal in its opposite, it is a mistake to permit coldness to stop one's heart from yearning.

C.

When we first met, the season was late summer. In the present, the seasons continue to change but with each transition you remain control-group constant. At that time, the reason had yet to be revealed; now with late summer turned to mid-fall, we live able to peer back and observe the chaos in the bullring as a receding crucible, nothing more, our reason resonant in our regard one for the other.

Back then, our lifetimes were waiting patiently to be more fully lived. It is incredible to think how many years can pass and yet patience endures. There is no Strange door to climb through, no Endgame to snap us out of or into the reality we thought we should have, could have, *must* have, lived. There is only the now. Your strides are short and mighty, your clutch ironclad and gripping. As you teach, you bind and mesh to maintain vital connections. Grown accustomed to environs filled with pontification, you welcome the knowledge I have always carried with the altruistic motivation of helping a peer.

When mentor and pupil switch places, the universe shares a supernova with the earth. With exquisite reason, in all seasons, the flash in the vacuum of the great beyond floods remembrances and actions for a lifetime. Our reactions never cease to ignite imaginations to drive creative juices in constant flow.

Christ, we have so much further yet to go. §

E.

Ecstasy: 1. a state of being overpowered by emotion, as by joy, grief, or passion: an ecstasy of delight 2. a feeling of overpowering joy; great delight; rapture 3. a trance, esp. one resulting from religious fervor 4. [usually E-] SLANG an illegal, mildly psychedelic derivative of amphetamine, CHNO, that slows down reactions and thought; MDMA

Repression is an asshole.

For years you remained closed off, unable to be induced to open up and be pleasantly shocked at how quickly you'd find relief. I knew what you kept penned up inside and assumed brilliance behind the curtain. I was going on a few drumskins of evidence though I couldn't be certain. Submersed in the new Anglo — that Pict habitude in Algonquin hills — you became vital with expressiveness, drunk on sonic energy, a giddy Davis disciple with improvisational flair that let nature take its course like it spat between slats of your muddy York retractable roof. Then, like a turtle too long exposed, you sank back into your shell and hoarded your sensation for yourself.

What caused you to lock your talents away was unknown to me, but I was persuaded that if you would only let your Rapunzel braids out, there'd be streams of gold aplenty to enrich the world. Your coming-out party, I reckoned, would be a Tour de La Force and not the Grimm expedition you figured it must be. Mind filled with fairy tales, convinced the creative experience held no new lessons, you exhibited a childlike refusal to taste the morsel you'd never previously experienced yet conclusively pronounced unconsumable. Arms crossed, you shot little-boy-broken-dump-truck pouts in my direction and swore you'd never co-operate.

Then I surreptitiously blended the nutrients into your fruit-sweet treats. You ate it all up, never suspecting anything was amiss until the truth was revealed to you halfway through the meal. I observed with satisfaction a wreath of surprise in the "This-doesn't-taste-so-bad" expression that decorated your face like Christmas tinsel. It told me that this was the moment you finally saw your gift.

What is seen cannot magically become unseen, and the scene where you first witnessed revelation became the genesis for your words to fill a promising book full of captivating chapters. You chuckled at my clever deception, applauded my stubborn persistence, because your body and mind told you that now that you'd sampled the sugar high, you'd crave it for a lifetime.

Dispensing with the spoon I'd used to feed you your own truth, you cup the bowl in both palms and lift it to your lips while I gape at the other circular edge, questing to find your forehead. Things will never be the same after this, in the best possible way. Let's dig in.

From that moment until now, you've pursued every available avenue, medalled in every dumpster dive, and livened up every party under heaven to vocalize your next hit. When you sojourned to distant climes to scale mountains, each successive climb gave a new sense of the constellation of possibilities at your disposal. And even after one such (mis)adventure broke your ability to scale every towering staircase to project beauty in the meals you create, you returned home spiritually healed, prepared for recommencement on soils of origin. Having cultivated on three continents, to reap the harvest was to feed the world.

We developed new fields of fertility where young shoots clamoured for sunlight and sustenance, grew relentlessly in pools left behind by torrential rains, and flourished under the expertise of numerous sets of trained hands. For these labour-intensive tasks, we were fortunate to have all hands on deck, no questions asked, belief in the project strong yet confidence in the outcome maddeningly uncertain. The resources we applied to the farmlands we tilled were top-notch — our harvest came much earlier, the bounty much healthier, than either of us could have ever anticipated. Faces filled with pleasure and sculpted by genuinely delighted shock at sensations our produce delivered made every ounce of toil and trouble worth our exertions.

Excelling in the face of denigration and vapid underestimation has delightful mouthfeel.

Throughout these challenge-filled times, we remained connected and collectively capable, never to be Deere caught in headlights fatally unable to hightail it out of danger at a moment's notice. Seasons changed and those with permits to claim hides got to work — lock, stock, and barrel. Your assured successes at husbandry came despite all efforts to hang your antlers on the wall. It was astonishing the speed with which the wild animal viewed from a respectful distance became prey that hunters sought to turn into a trophy for sport and self-satisfied boasting. No matter that the murder of dreams is reprehensible, once convinced the buck was full of pestilent excrement, there weren't any shots left that could lead to continued carefree living.

You fled and I followed in hot pursuit, exercised by those who felt chasing you off the field would exorcise the demons that haunted their memories. In the heat of the chase, I had no idea why they so desperately wanted to spill your blood. When I eventually caught up and was finally able to explore the scene, I realized their discovery was as valid as Cristobal Colombo's claims to the New World. We come from peoples whose DNA understand what exploitation means — entrapment to the cellular level, no hope for cultural escape, destruction of lifestyles, devastation of ecologies. No way, my deer, you did not cave to their depressions and understood the difference between the forest and the trees. Fresh air fed your fire, enabled you to accelerate after the brush with branches of their ideology.

Expression in the face of repression is a life-saving act.

Real life is never a fairy tale and new lessons aplenty instruct your continuously evolving creative experience. I am pleasantly relieved at how quickly you overcame the shock. Your little-boy-broken-dump-truck pouts have been replaced by gratitude and you swore you'd never co-operate. Surprise in the "this-doesn't-taste-so-bad" expression that came to dominate your features has been replaced with a knowing appreciation. Sweetness can be bitter but your stomach for digesting the sour and turning it into fuel for new fields of fertility now transmits to your seed, grown to fruit, destined to feed the world. Your elevation to expert in husbandry complete, you stand prepared to enjoy the produce of your bounty as you expand your positive impact on the land, for the benefit of many more young shoots below the soil, just waiting to break through.

The resources you apply to the farmlands you till are top-notch. Continue to excel at what you do, every bit of it worth your ample exertions. Let nature take its course beyond the fences of your fields.

And allow each set of hands to reap what they sow. §

O!

Obstinate: 1. unreasonably determined to have one's own way; not yielding to reason or plea; stubborn; dogged; mulish 2. resisting remedy or treatment: an obstinate fever 3. not easily subdued, ended, etc.

It's remarkable yet karmically unsurprising that you show up as third in a consecutive series of letters that denotes the person who's in charge. You've infrequently worn that title at your progressive and impactful stops along the way, though without doubt, you are often pulling the strings. Whether others are aware or not, your will be done, and your word is bond.

You proliferate best in mushroom mimicry, steadily increasing in value and sustaining power below the radar, in the shadow of tall trees that command all the attention atop your nature's vistas, ready and able to feed others. Despite small stature and a perceived position of inferiority on the food chain, your nutritional composition packs a powerful punch. You're able to sprout in whatever form is needed to suit your environment — sometimes you pop up as a tasty delight, other times a poisonous threat to the uninitiated, still other times capable of providing an intoxicatingly good time.

Though it's obvious that you cannot be mistaken for a fun guy.

The nature of many of the challenges you face skirts logic and reason, and coats the travails that you need to address, even as the people around you try to bring you to heel. You are infuriated by being viewed as a secondary characteristic but have leaned into it, keeping abreast of any development to make it your own. Something about producing a Tom Collins with lemons and talent informed your modus operandi after surviving a plethora of sour patches. Can-do attitude mixed with acid wit and the hopeful seed of something better are embedded and ever-present at your core.

When you first showed me your power of persuasion, I was the safe arbour you pined for in the hope I'd provide the shade required for you to conjure your magic. Ours became a symbiotic relationship where you played quietly competent producer to my temperamental loudmouth director. My strengths came through best onstage while you made sure the lights were on, the cameras rented, and the action made available to as large an audience as possible. Without you, my bark lacked the bite needed to build anything long-term or sustainable. In every subsequent step of your life, you've laid a plank upon which others can stand tall and speak loudly. You betrayed nothing in your polite applause from the wings. Yet without you, how could any of this ever hope to fly?

Compromise has long been a fickle friend you'd rather disassociate with permanently. When you initially employed it to aid in crawling progressively forward, you pulled deliverables out of the crab bucket of jealous inequity, and they pulled you out with them. It's a helpful advancement to get the job done; you're less crabby outside the bucket than in it. Others quickly learned your ways, came to respect your quick intuition, hard shell, and sharp claws, and got the hell out of the way to give you room to latch onto the big man's shirttails and never let go. Left to your own devices, grateful for the allergies that keep people from trying to eat you for lunch, your stubborn attachment to the pace of the place now makes letting go a maddeningly self-jeopardizing choice. Eventually, you tire of sideways crawling and become overwhelmed with the urge to fall off and run in a totally different direction.

Even a crafty stowaway knows when shifting to a different mode of transport will serve them better than where they are latched at any given moment. Typically, you've made those choices impeccably. Not always, though.

Due to being strong-willed, you sometimes drive pilfered repurposed conveyances deep into accumulated snow to try and plough through, then get stuck with tires spinning. When you've needed a tow truck to extract you from crises of your own making, you've usually had everything on hand that you needed to avoid being trapped there for long. Learning to appreciate the benefits of being forced into solitary frozenness is not always quickly recognized, but they are present all the same. Rear-view mirror musings about past pains, screams at the windshield about bygone fraught tropical adventures, cursing at forgetting to ensure you were speeding off on season-appropriate tires — all come and go, and in their wake is a winter-wonderful sun reflecting silver shimmer-smooth expanses of snowflakes on trees and houses and abandoned, stranded cars. Take a beat, a breath, every so often, and take stock of the blessing in/of the blizzard. Headstrong determination to do what others couldn't, and failing spectacularly, is still not a good enough reason to leave your vehicle behind.

No matter the challenges in the terrain, you constantly advance apace. You find satisfaction in the traction of action. And you're always cooking.

Perfection is a dish you continuously attempt but are never able to match exactly to the recipe, even when you've added mushroom to give the meal's profile its best flavour. You defiantly bang pots and pans, sully utensils, utilize culinary machinery with precise skill, and heat up the oven and stovetop to impressive effect. But not even you can stomach the unachievable. Long before you could even attempt to get a taste, that dish ran away from you with the spoon. You might be a chief executive in your own kitchen, but you cannot make the entire universe dance marionette-like until your will be done. Even though you never stop trying.

You always carry yourself like a boss.

Oh, do you ever. §

K.

Kind: 1. sympathetic, friendly, gentle, tender-hearted, generous, etc. 2. cordial: kind regards 3. ARCHAIC loving; affectionate 4. OBS. natural; native

The first time we set eyes upon each other, mutual recognition of potential realities twinned with a shared passion for mining the riches of diamonds. The fundamentals were innate to me, the strategic manipulation of the implements for success a personal superpower for you. Resourcefulness has defined the industry of our efforts ever since. With skills as underdeveloped as our minds, we learned together about striking rock with picks, about weighing material substance and shaping it for higher order uses to make us wealthy beyond measure. For many of the intervening years, your focus turned you into a crack social experimenter with a Nobel winner's flair for method. You learned your lessons much better than I did, your facility for mathematics as clear as mine was not, and from then to now those talents, honed over decades, turned you into a mental magnate.

Thankfully, you never hammered me for my deficiencies but always pointed me in the direction of my north star.

You were too good at everything to not notice my strengths. With parallel devotion to excellence, though excavating separate and unique tunnelling sites, we both became expert analyzers of what was in the ground before us. You, knee-deep in the muck, pulled from it, forged it, and applied it with the grace and precision of a practiced artisan even as the messiness around you surged upwards to swallow you until it reached your waist. In contrast, I described it in terms that flowed like groundwater that was liberated from a fissure in an underground reservoir, satisfying those who thirsted for creative refreshment. Your talent is stultifying at scale, towering at magnitude, and astounding to absorb in a single take. Tower power personified.

From your heights, you tune new frequencies like radio waves to iterate new innovations to help solve intractable problems. Wherever you go to work your wizardry, the news you generate is steadily revelatory, readily relatable, and reliably groundbreaking. Over years, you've transmitted transoceanic tremors, operated under the shade of tropical palms, planted ascending roots like Black Forest pine, fir, and spruce, spun like a Ferris wheel on the shoreline of royally significant waterways while cultivating change at every touchdown on foreign soils. You collect memories and experiences like washed-up holiday keepsake rocks wrought from coral on a Quintana Roo coastline.

Dreams do eventually come true, mine and yours.

K.

No person is an island, but some are archipelagoes of potent possibilities. You are a hodgepodge of disparate energies shooting off in various directions, a living megawatt brainstorm of near-nuclear proportions that can power a city just as easily as destroy it in a single freak flash of meltdown mania. Somehow, you have always made harnessing your volts look like kindergartners breezily building Lego sets just after emerging refreshed from nap time. Internal bridges that carry your trains of thought from intellectual place to place shuttle infinite railcars with cognitive motherlodes with just-on-time acuity that startles the senses of the uninitiated. If Haley Joel Osment sees dead people, your sixth sense is in snatching new life from unseen decay before the core of the rot brings it all crashing down.

You could have chosen a simpler way to exist but to spawn your legacy you have to salmon swim upstream. Without the crashing currents in your face, you would find it tough to feel alive.

Since returning from your Da Gama global gambolling, you chose to stop messing about and get stable. On the first go-round, you traded in staples only to end up navigating the perils of an extended shitstorm to eventually find safe harbour. The second time around, searching for glory and birthing a cape(r) of good hope *con tus dias*, after surviving the storms the voyage revealed what you were searching for, even though you didn't know its importance when you set off on your original embarkation. Up in the crow's nest, you feathered your own perch sufficiently to need no other assistance to raise your young; it mattered little that your path looked nothing like that of your compatriots. All that mattered was where you found yourself at the end of your exploratory journeys.

It is a testament to your internal fortitude that you command the coastline from an impregnably redoubtable station, ready to repel any hostile assault. The positioning is necessary though your disposition would rather situate you amongst the people, at the edges of the crowd but part of the action, engaged on your own terms, sharing joy and goodwill at every turn. Having survived your share of skirmishes with armies guided by dastardly intentions, you have never stopped being able and willing to accept others under attack within the walls of your formidable fortress. In general, they find you prepared with the basic training to lead and the self-command to effectively comfort those under your care. Protecting the occupants comes naturally to a person accustomed to hard labour; repelling enemies at the point of the sword without losing any foot soldiers along the way is a hallmark of your excellence.

Sometimes, the greatest kindnesses can be gleaned in moments of heightened anxiety, honed *in extremis*, and given back as compassionate testimony to the beauty of human ingenuity and resourcefulness. Though you find yourself making the same kinds of choices that O did, in finding a way to stow your apprehensions and still forge ahead promisingly from a place of empathy and understanding speaks to your irresistible interpersonal competence.

When bonded, friendship forms fast and is titanium strong. No time, space, or circumstance can successfully corrode it. Through all kinds of weather, the mettle of our mutual excavations endures. You may have always been better at math but even I can equate your generosity of spirit with the hard-won wisdom of your wanderings. In the eyes of the tested, one can find the answers to the examination and feel confident with the room given to see what you know.

Flying colours hold no mysteries for you. §

X.

Expectation: 1. a looking forward to; anticipation 2. a looking for as due, proper, or necessary 3. a thing looked forward to 4. [also pl.] a reason or warrant for looking forward to something; prospect for the future, as of advancement or prosperity 5. the probability of the occurrence, duration, etc. of something, esp. as indicated by statistics

Rarest of figures amongst the most difficult to define, you as a character may be easy to draw but never simple to describe. Hence the shape and sound of the words I use here roll differently than those that precede and follow them. In unexaggerated phrases and direct language, I hope to reach you where you slumber.

How does someone begin to extol your excellence, to expand on the extraordinary ways your place in my heart exceeds your prominence in my mind? To extrapolate from the emigrations and the self-expansions you experienced at the expense of your energies, we engender exemplary respect and exuberant admiration from our extended branches, exultant about your exodus from the place of your birth to the place of ours.

Emblem of critical crossroads, implement of illiteracy, symbol of the unknown, your dexterity and versatility stand out when one examines how you branded your inheritors with your values and proclivities. Yours was the strongest soul I've ever known, with a body physically capable of pound-for-pound feats that would shame larger men. Yet you were also hard as stone in mindset and determined to provide the very best for your family. The sear scorch crispy at the tip of your imprint belied a gentleness that was just as able to mark others as a brand that burns skin deep. Flame fails to impact me in the way your quietest words shook my existence to the core from the first moment you uttered them to this moment where they echo in the recesses of my most treasured recollections. The reverberations disturb any tendencies towards inertia and jolt me forward in honour of my own capabilities, fully realized.

For an example of what love looks like at its most alluring, one only needed to witness your handling of any interpersonal interaction. The exquisite understanding of emotion, the self-control, the deceptively cowled appearance of whip-strong intensity that seemed to materialize out of nowhere — you set a standard and expected it to unfailingly be met, without appearing overbearing or excessive in your expressions.

You learned to use your hands to earn a place in foreign lands to become a tradesman; you laid foundations beneath our feet that were sturdy and well constructed, able to bear the weight of multiple generations. You installed the cabinetry to house and support our dreams at a level where we never lost sight of them and built bars both for the service of alcohol and to extend as measuring sticks to clear with our aspirations. None that came after you could find the space to excel if you hadn't first fabricated the rooms where we grew into ourselves. Most literally, those rooms sprouted from former farmlands fertilized with the seeds of immigrant dreams to extract crops of new citizens prepared to leave their mark. These latter-day pioneers with their little houses in the woods, or on the prairie, or in the centres of suburbia, started off wilder and ended up with heritage hours broadcast to enlighten on the matter of Black lives. If only you could see now just how much your Herculean efforts to establish yourself as an expatriate of sun and sand created men and women in exceptional demand.

Every success at our hands is an exhortation to you, patriarch, as deliverer of our sustenance and spirit.

Yours was the only personality that fit the definition of "dad" in my childhood and adolescence, the only father figure worthy of the name. I carry the damage of those days deep in my bones, unable to be exhumed, covered by crushing layers of sedimentary sentiments long buried in my psyche. The spinoffs of genetic strands cycle exposed and exasperatingly efficient into cellular inheritances passed forward. Decades yet to be exhibited afflicted with existential dreads braided into their molecular composition. Despite these disruptive truths, you embraced me with the warmth of an equatorial summer every time your eyes exclaimed their joy at drawing in my silhouette, irradiated by your brilliance. You had the power to reduce my fear and apprehension so it could reach no higher into my lived experience than the floor planks you shaped from fallen forests. You showed me how to tread carefully across the terrain of my traumas and regrets and still find solid enough footing to make a way that was worthy of the trek.

As a minor, I learned from you what little I gathered of the exoskeletal nature of masculinity. Your interventions showed me how to cultivate a more humanitarian iteration of manhood that serves better in the real world. My first steps into those realities were guided by your patient hand, ready to help if needed but present mostly to make sure that any fall wasn't overly painful or unendurable. Lessons came in bite sizes large enough to fortify but small enough to digest. You filled me up over time, hoping that I could use these teachings well, determined not to live life on my behalf but to hold up a mirror to my growth that I could not look away from and ignore any blemishes or bruises, hoping they'd disappear on their own, no exfoliant or balm required.

When we all gathered inside the enclave you fashioned with your hands, you took pride in what you saw while feeling little need to overwhelm or dominate proceedings. Yours was a quiet form of dominion, benevolent yet exacting, where silence could not be taken for granted as unspoken consent. Your ways were known and well understood, with no need for you to overtly exert your will or your power. Yours was a loving strength that permeated every corner of every space, filled us all, touched us all. The reassurance of clearly communicated boundaries and innately discernable rules — when they would be forcefully applied, and situations where exceptions may be made — wrapped us like a blanket during a late-night Netflix marathon.

Little did we know that you carried damage deep in your bones, about to be excavated, clandestinely covered by crushing layers of innocent ignorance about to be exposed to the harshness of the elements of our familial reality.

One day, a checkup on a presumed physical injury turned out to be a bill coming due that ushered you unexpectedly towards the checkout. It didn't fully register until I saw you there — reluctantly in line, set to pay the final cash-out price and depart on less-than-agreeable terms. Antiseptic environs set up to commemorate a centenary of memories spurred a recalled flood of our own about a man who had gradually revealed himself over an expanse three-quarters as long. We all wanted to put our fears to bed, but quickly realized that the only bed in a room not constructed by any form of your conception was a measuring stick. It could not extend our dreams for you at a level where would be able to maintain sight of them for much longer. We were on vigil, agonized by your agonies, waiting to exhale while choking on every one of our own breaths. Excruciating.

The fade from a body physically capable of pound-for-pound feats that would shame larger men to the hollowed-out husk of loose skin, diminished flesh, exhausted eyes, and marrowless bones we stood guard over in your last days still hurts. An inexorable descent into a cancerously painful exit endures as a canker forever unhealed on my heart.

You deserved so much better for the ways you made so many other lives so much better.

The last time I was at your gravesite, I examined the raised letters, numbers, symbols, and images that marked your final resting place. Standing there with family, looking upon you at rest with Q by your side — precious treasure reunited with the strongest soul I've ever known — I expelled a prayer of thanksgiving. The two most important examples of what it means to lead an exemplary existence, excellence personified, filled me with an excess of emotion that spilled from ducts. Tears that tear at my heart every time I think of you found freedom that day. I hope they found you too.

For in your earthly absence, I can still find your temporal persistence in the glint of a cousin's eye, the wisdom flowing from an uncle's tongue, the reverence with which your constructions are held by us all. You helped to build me beautifully with the sweat of your brow and the skill of your dexterous hands. I would exchange those memories with your presence any day. But with each excavation of my deepest feelings, I always find you there — exultant, exquisite, exhilarated by what your family continues to become. I truly hope these words reach you where you slumber. §

H.

Hunger: 1. the discomfort, pain, or weakness caused by a need for food; famine; starvation 2. a desire, need, or appetite for food 3. any strong desire; craving

Beginnings are delicate moments, rife with chances to misunderstand and hopelessly tangle what could otherwise be smoothly cordial relations for a lifetime. I was not present at your dawning, but once you started to attain altitude, I was able to be a participant in the game. Gaining skills allowed you to play for keeps in defence of a goal you had to pitch across a field of possibility, all in the hope you would score the top opportunity for victory.

Plugging into the amplifier of your aptitudes required years of work on both your parts, commitments of both your hearts, refusal of transplants and grafts to stay steady in your space, knowing that, cultivated properly, success could be explosive. Stick to it and drill the craft to sample the steps taken towards mastery, one failure at a time, leading to improvement, then more achievement, then to expertise. Mix the products of your explorations like a multi-track pro loop, whether on a computer or on the sporting landscape, followed by fans starving to savour your triumphs. Many hours of labour led to a special day when a parade of opportunities found their way down your main avenue, championing your electrified potential. Once the benefits of the flavours in your concoctions started coming your way, you drank them in like municipally sourced spring water, and charged a premium to profit from your own self-development.

Like a brown-skinned Angelica Schuyler soprano singing Hamiltonian Miranda melodies, you have never been satisfied. Whether it was with a bowl of opportunity drowned in marinara partnered with pork and beef meatballs or after finishing off a kick against the referee penalized, twine snapped back by a Beckham-like hook shot placed perfectly inside a tall cylindrical post, you always know exactly what you want. And crave it. And know how to make it delicious when you acquire it.

I've heard it said that the best way to a man's heart is through his stomach. If this is true in your case, then it can be no surprise that your intestinal gateways yawn somnolently as if arising from deep slumber, with the passions of your pursuits running towards doorways at top speed. All the people in your lives that you wanted to prevent from getting there never believed your attempts to dissuade or distract. They always knew the way, and despite yourselves, you've always eaten it up.

You both have consumed some of the greatest loves while ending up with gastritis inflamed by emotional detritus.

There is a deep rumble that moves you to lamentation when your bellies are empty, and an unexpected feeling of fullness during times of bounty. I remind you — eat at a reasonable pace and know what you are bringing into your body. If it's not feeding you, then dispense as quickly as possible with the empty calories. Work out the excesses and trim the fat so that you can digest all that is good that the world has to offer to you. A bit of roughage is a good thing, so don't skimp on the fibre meant to keep you in regular connection with what you wish to put out into the universe.

Don't make a meal of this. Maintain contact with your inner self and make music that moves the world.

Over the years, you've come full circle while additionally finding your way in the 6ix — an irony that mirrors the spread of days that separated your arrivals one from the other. Your advents like holiday celebrations signalled that you were destined to be cosmic partners on your rocket ride up the charts. While one produces sounds that form the backdrop of a generation, the other feeds their souls while whipping them into shape. You were always able to personally train your sights on the bigger picture, hustling to sate the cravings that would otherwise go unfulfilled.

Never interested in a front, you orient towards an expressway travelling into verdant fields, the gardeners with implements of productivity that harvest the incredible mentalities you possess in spades. Being green does not always mean being taken for a ride fuelled by ignorance. Your ethanol is the experiences you carry from the moments of disappointment, the memories of lack, the desire to create and gain and grow — to press power from what you cobble together from your stock of mental motivations leaves others with less ability to tap into their wells in the dust.

Back at the start, you were pint-sized accompaniment for a keg full of courageous folks who wanted nothing better than to guide you in the right direction. Now, as the life of the party, feeding the masses as a chef of dreams and rocking the crowd from DJ booths, pleasure maximizers, I sense that you can still dance in sync to explode the minds of those forming the circle but never brave enough to be centred. If music be the food of love, play on — and if you be the feeders from the tweeters, the drawers of the bassline, the chefs cooking up this night of nights, then please don't stop the music.

Such hungers are ravenous, and I know you both got the soup. §

W.

Worry: 1. a) to harass or treat roughly with or as with continual biting or tearing with the teeth: a dog worrying a bone b) to pluck at, push on, touch, etc. repeatedly in a nervous or determined way: worrying the loose tooth with his tongue 2. to annoy, bother, harass, vex, etc. 3. to cause to feel troubled or uneasy; make anxious; distress

At first, it did not seem possible that the shipwreck contained anything salvageable. Wrenched from the rocky seabed like a rusted nut secured to an abandoned pier, hoisted aloft under the glare of a cold late-day light, there was no breath left to animate any further episodes in the aftermath of the destruction. The carcass stank of missed opportunities, misunderstood signals, misplaced hopes, mistaken self-identities. The hook that bore its weight no longer bristled with the same devastating sharpness it once held. The chain that connected hook to pulley bore grooves, nicks, wear, and tear of ocean storms from seasons past. Time erodes all things and nothing that travels through surf and sea is capable of self-repair.

Perhaps if greater attention had been paid both to the integrity of the vessel and navigation through turbulent waters, it would not have found itself at the centre of an avoidable disaster.

However, there are times when it is possible to reclaim purpose out of the wreckage. With attention, what seemed like large irreparable gashes turn to small tears, resolution to simply patch over certain spots without deep discussion of the damages therein, our agreement to share the cost of repairing what is left of what once was leaves space for new buoyancy, albeit on the rise and fall of different tides.

After the experiences I had with your hull, I became a willing and dedicated landlubber. You may sail on with a different skipper but at least I am assured that you will answer my call should the crackle of your CB drift across the (air) waves with tales and testimonies to share. That grants relief less nuanced than a map of the terrain I happily inhabit, and that you've grown comfortable bypassing. I'm grateful I found a safer place to land.

The solidity beneath my feet is less concerning than the vagaries of our existence that pull you hither and yon; on the surface, you appear placid and positively responsive, yet you are poised to move with the crosswind on a moment's notice and ride out its wild ways like Stampede steer in a foothill frolic. It becomes exhausting to be battered constantly with gale-force consternation — a tempest largely of your own making, yet one that must be endured to get anywhere at all. Much of the bluster buffets unendingly, fails to satisfy once one is finally able to reach its end, and creates so much waste, one feels tossed and trashed in the aftermath. I'd gorged excessively and wanted nothing more than to empty myself of its worst effects.

Like cancerous tropics you were on a steady boil, heated in perennial preparation for when leaves become departures from your expectations. Drowning them and setting them to steep in your steamed energies, you forced the truth of their contents into a cauldron of your seething conception. Sweetened with your syrupy sentiments and milked for everything they were worth, once dunked into the simmering brew it was impossible to emerge without a lasting impact from the scalding. It is impossible to live an extended lifetime in such an environment, and I yearned for a more soothing concoction that required less energy to fabricate and was much cooler to imbibe.

I became intolerant of the prospect of burning my tongue repeatedly in the liquid fury covered in froth that you kept placing before me and so, out of self-preservation, bid *olé* to the café. Nor did I wish to concern myself overmuch with the prospect of spilled tea, and so removed myself from range of the whispers. Perhaps the steeping would be too potent for your easy consumption, or rich cream added in error instead of skimmed milk would ruin the flavour and disgust the sensibilities of any descendent of a former British colonist within reasonable vicinity. Every potential hazard loomed like an airship in full flight, strangling the light with lofty disasters. Hot air threatened my every prospect for success, exploding every attempt to connect with my inspirations.

After I chose to depart the shores that had done so much to drain my capital and arrest my forward progress for no good reason, deeper understanding of the source of your rambunctious roar blew through my relocated front door. Control is a sailcloth as fictitious as a Linus linen, yet the yearning to grab hold of it leaches from you like saline contaminants. Saltiness explained is no easier to fully digest.

I was never made for a leashed life subject to the whims of another's unattainable standards of safety and security. The world is inherently a treacherous place and the reason why movements must be both measured and bold. The contrast held in balance makes for slick stepping stones.

I, however, refuse to be paralyzed by fear of slipping.

While time erodes all things and nothing that travels through surf and sea is capable of self-repair, we are always able to find a new harbour and start over again. Gratitude exudes for the reconstructed state in which we now dwell, but I relish the control I have in my wave to you as you sail by, my arm lifted at my own behest, giving in its sentiment yet distant enough to exert no direct influence. I can share my joy at your adventures under my own terms while sparing nary a thought to the concerns that guide your navigations.

From the safety of my station, I pick up the handheld radio, raise it to my mouth, and press the button. Over and out. §

G.

Gratitude: a feeling of thankful appreciation for favors or benefits received; thankfulness

You were the unexpected blessings in a world that treats me as darkly as the continent of our ancestry. You, blessed with the melanated misunderstanding that is bred into our skin without an ounce of compassion for our wish to be seen as human and not as a colour, must find your own way through the labyrinth, march boldly forward. The light that ignited as you came into being continues to follow you at every turn, dampened by red carpeted footfalls step after step after step. Though you can't see the pathway clearly just yet, it remains there, in latent expectation like Michael Jackson paved street squares, waiting for your weight to trigger illumination of your brilliance.

When you burst onto the scene, I hoped to lay waste vindictive and stereotypical insinuations about the freshness of meat wrapped with a similar organ to the one that encases me. Encases you too. The persistence and perniciousness of the negative reviews, based on nothing but the biases of the belligerent, at first made me think them jealous of us at our grooviest. Rather, it came true to me as blindingly obvious as a Rodney King beating that the only groove determined fit to our purpose is the one we fit into at the end of the road. When I reflect on some of the first sounds at volume that you ever heard, I recall that they were the strains of music composed from a multiplicity of multicultural sonic collisions. Synthesizing the Caribbean reggae and calypso, African soukous, and American jazz and R&B performed within your muffled earshot, layered with hip-hop and spoken word, was a multiethnic grouping of stage players tied together in melodic and harmonic ecstasy.

Still, I can't let go of the belief that where you exist in the shade of judgment, a less harsh one than the one attached to me will be bestowed upon you. Caramel is preferable in the grand flow of things. Chocolate is best in (behind) bars.

My fear is that in your yearning for acceptance in a world not always kind to your kind, you'll discover that your value is not treasured like the purest gold but buried like our history in underfunded archives, mould-infested basement trunks, dusty attics, and long-forgotten photo albums. To allow them to forget is to remove any basis upon which forgiveness could find purchase. To buy peace, the obstinate gatekeepers who worry about keeping "us in our place" must be cleared away. To make room for what you bring to bear is a grizzly task that our brown-toned predecessors in this polar place have achieved with their dignity and self-respect intact. You are the bearers of the lit torches of their legacies. We must trust you and your compatriots with the task of keeping their flames burning bright in every place where their transformational bonfires lit up our country.

We know you will not disappoint your ancestors.

I would be unsurprised to see such a situation leave you with an overwhelming feeling of uncertain anxiety. These characters on these pages are penned in part to prevent your past from becoming predeceased, banished to perdition, before the zealous succeed at imparting this stifled wisdom into the hearts and minds of your generation and those to follow. There is a modern hunger for these stories, the ones that speak to our beauty beyond your colour — there will be eternal regret if we fail to burn them into the surface of our national mythology before our brand cools to frigidity in a snowbank on a downtown Ottawa street. The matter of our lives is a breathing and sentient lamentation for societal sins of the past, the naughty acts of illicit historic subjugation and exploitation the soundtrack of your rouge-cushioned forward movements. Lyrics as terse as they are insistent, anger infused, and demanding.

Change is needed, but dollars are required to make change possible. Make sure your demands always have mint conditions.

Your quarrel is not with the past, but with the present; you and yours must seize your status from the grasp of intolerant sanctimony to create blessed space for the requirements of what is yet to come. You hold this task in talented hands that know how to craft something gorgeous and animate beauty from whatever raw materials are placed in your palms. For this reason alone, your future is not a land of trepidation and fear in my imaginings. In fact, your future should await your arrival with breathless anticipation.

When united, the two of you shall be unstoppable.

At this point, there is nothing left but gratitude.

Struggle in this life is as beautiful as Talib Kweli rapped about, as Ta-Nehisi Coates wrote in his memoir, as Buddha philosophized as the basis of his ancient truth. Without it, in its absence and with the prevalence of ease on the streetscape of my existence, you never come to be. In the absence of my run through the gauntlet, my brick would never have been placed to support the edifice our community builds every day that is meant to stand the test of time. Without the work the struggle forced upon my shoulders and the institutional repression meant to hold me back permanently, my breakthroughs large and small could not stand as monuments of my love for you and my desire to see you have a better life than the one that I inherited from my forebears.

Beginning life with a deep breath story threadbare connection to my first successful inhalation makes me grateful for every moment that has come since. The number of n-bombs hurled in my direction could detonate Halifax

Harbour and level the city all over again, and yet, I remain grateful. My ferocity and instinctive awareness of from where and how bullshit comes at me, which has prepared me to defend against it from any angle, is a surprising blessing borne of fear, frustration, disillusionment, and a deep-seated anger that can never be fully dispelled. Even so, every extreme disappointment, stolen opportunity, ignored indignity, illegal incident, discriminatory destruction, fight for fairness, and racist reaction was, and is, a chance to say thank you.

The main reason for this, you might ask with a puzzled twist to your pretzel-salted visage?

Because you are the product of the struggle.

This pen that memorializes you on these pages is the struggle giving birth to new generations of resistance, persistence, strength, integration, differentiation — we are part of the whole and a whole other part. We live on a code-switched doubly conscious invisible plane, holding a prism through which we must refract any light shone upon us to find any kind of a rainbow to bring us joy. No matter how much folks who exist as we do wish away the plane, it's plain that its complexities and contradictions will always dictate how we are viewed. So, if we cannot forge rainbows out of our shine, we may be deprived of it entirely, and consigned to the shadows.

My mind wobbles and my world spins when I think too hard about how you will impact this ball of rock, wind, water, ice, and dirt. Of one thing I am certain, however: You are too much light to be dimmed, my sweet. Shine on and paint the town red with your every pace.

The light that ignited as you came into being continues to follow you at every turn. You create rainbows at every place you touch. Because you are not the plane, nor the prism.

You *are* the light. With our gratitude, shine on — and make us proud. §

Acknowledgements

I want to express my deepest gratitude, first of all, to Kwame Scott Fraser, who was the publisher at Dundurn when my book idea was first accepted. From that moment forward, he has been incredibly supportive and freely offered me his constant encouragement, unflagging friendship, and wise counsel. He even went so far as to arrange a writing coach, Reed Jones, to whom I also owe a heartfelt thanks for his clarity of perspective, sardonic wit, literary suggestions, and belly laughs during phone calls on drives around Halifax and in our text messages. I look forward to future Jamaican adventures with both of you.

Many thanks to the team at Dundurn Press / Rare Machines who helped me shepherd this project from inception to publication (most especially, in addition to Kwame, thanks to Erin Pinksen, Meghan Macdonald, Chris Houston, Natasha

Kempnich, Laura Boyle, and Rajdeep Singh). Without your steadfast belief in what I was creating and the reassurance that it was a project worth executing, I'm not sure I would have finished it. Particular thanks to Erin, who stayed with me through the difficult times at the start and near the finish of the writing, kept on assuring everyone inside Dundurn that they were going to love what I did when it was done, and who kept feeding me positive reinforcement in the darkest moments of what was a very bumpy, challenge-filled journey to the finish line. You can be my hype woman anytime!

Extra special kudos to my editor, Peter Midgley, who is honestly one of the easiest people in the world to work with on my words and thoughts. By the end, he could basically read my artistic mind — not a healthy habit to develop! His laid-back, firm approach and willingness to slaughter sacred cows, coupled with his witticisms and sagacity, made the process a delight. I'm honoured to now call him a friend. Without input from your exquisitely sublime mind, this would have ended up being a far inferior book than what it eventually became. This triumph is a shared one. *Merci mille fois.*

I also wanted to express my gratitude to other friends and peers who helped me along the way, read parts of the book and gave useful feedback, and generally kept me moving in the right direction so that *Alphabet Soup* could come to fruition: my mentor and harshest/kindest literary critic,

George Elliott Clarke; my partner in *AfriCANthology* crime, Nathan Fréchette; my writing buddies Ray Guillermo, Ashley Bristowe, Devyani Saltzman, Amy McQuaid, and Raluca Balasa; West Coast writer/inspirer Amy McVay; my adopted little sister / fashionista kickass woman-about-town Hillary LeBlanc; my work buddy and comrade-at-EDI Sabrina Propper; creative couple extraordinaire Judith Shaw and Gary Kohut; and my longtime dear friend Natasha Cheff. All of you have been incredible to me along the journey, always having my back, never letting me fall, and always being super honest with what you felt about what I was doing with this project. You shared my excitement with me when I couldn't contain it in my own body, and picked me up in my darkest hours, and at times when I feared I couldn't push through and get this thing done. This book is a testament to the power of supportive friendship. Bless your hearts.

Warmest thank-yous to others who have been there to show love and support along the way: my PIN crew — Devyani, Shannon Litzenberger, Kevin Ornsby, Evalyn Parry, Kevin Loring, Leslie Ting, and Shary Boyle — my cousin and brother-in-song Paul Grossett; my younger siblings Kalaycia and Khamar McLeggon; my Jacksonville-based peeps Renée Richards-Carter and John Carter III; the entire Frankson-Pink-Oliver family complex on both sides of the Atlantic; and the innumerable poets, writers, and creative beings who had little pokes of encouragement, supportive comments, and thoughtful remarks to share along the way that helped me keep on keeping on. Though I was alone in my Covid-imposed isolation for large chunks of the creative period, and away from home at the end of it, the village still participated spiritedly in the raising of this child. I'm grateful for your generosity that allowed me to make completing this book, a major dream for my life, a reality.

Also, for those who have not otherwise been recognized in this note but nevertheless made their presence felt on this project, I also honour their aid and support. You know who you are. Thank you very much.

Of course, the subjects of the letters provided me with the inspiration to put these thoughts down on paper. For good, bad, and ugly reasons that you've already read, thank you for causing me to become who I am in large part due to the wide variety of experiences I went through with all of you (whether you recognize yourself as a subject in this book or not). May the passing of time bless each and every one of you still living with wisdom and imbue you with joy, tact, empathy, dignity, and grace. Lord knows — some of you need it more desperately than others.

And for those letter subjects who have transitioned from this world to the next, know that you are not forgotten, you are fiercely loved, and you are dearly and deeply missed.

Finally, to Chantal Le Faive: I love you, Green Girl. *Bisous bisous bisous!*

About the Author

Photo by LaughingWall Production

A. GREGORY FRANKSON is an educator, activist, public speaker, consultant, award-winning literary artist, and essayist based in Toronto, Canada.

Greg contributed to and edited the critically acclaimed *AfriCANthology: Perspectives of Black Canadian Poets* (Renaissance Press, 2022) and is the author of four poetry collections: *Cerebral Stimulation* (2006), *Lead on a Page* (2012), *A Weekly Dose of Ritallin* (2015), and *Cerebral Confections* (2021). His work also appears in five other anthologies: *African Leadership: Powerful Paradigms in the 21st Century* (2023), *Nothing Without Us Too* (2022), *The Great Black North* (2013), *That Not Forgotten* (2012), and *Mic Check: An Anthology of Canadian Spoken Word Poetry* (2008).

Greg is a former Canadian national poetry slam champion, an inaugural VERSe Ottawa Hall of Honour inductee, and past poet laureate of the International Initiative for Mental Health Leadership. He was also an on-air poetic commentator for CBC Radio One's *Here and Now Toronto.* His articles have appeared in publications like the *Globe and Mail*, the *Toronto Star*, All Lit Up, Rabble, and ByBlacks.com, amongst others.

Greg enjoys bike rides, hiking in the woods, his mom's stew peas and rice, and a lively debate amongst friends.

Alphabet Soup is Greg's first full-length work of creative non-fiction.